Graham
Crackers
Galoshes and
God

A LIGUORI POPULAR PERENNIAL

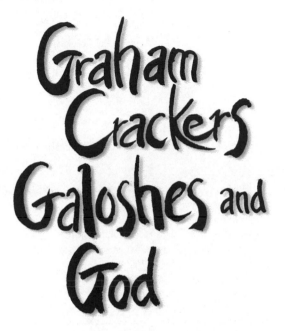

Graham Crackers Galoshes and God

**Everywoman's book
of cope and hope**

Bernadette McCarver Snyder

LIGUORI
PUBLICATIONS
One Liguori Drive
Liguori, MO 63057-9999

Published by Liguori Publications
Liguori, Missouri
www.liguori.org
www.catholicbooksonline.com

Library of Congress Cataloging-in-Publication Data

Snyder, Bernadette McCarver.
   Graham crackers, galoshes, and God : everywoman's book of cope and
hope / Bernadette McCarver Snyder.
      p.   cm.
   Essays selected from the author's Graham crackers, galoshes, and God
(c1982) and More graham crackers, galoshes, and God (c1985).
   "A Liguori popular perennial."
   ISBN 0-89243-778-2
   1. Women—Prayer books and devotions—English. 2. Christian life.
I. Title.
BV 4844.S64   1995   95-20243
242'.643—dc20

Essays in this edition selected and compiled from *Graham Crackers, Galoshes,
and God*, copyright © 1982 by Liguori Publications and *More Graham
Crackers, Galoshes, and God*, copyright © 1985 by Liguori Publications: both
by Bernadette McCarver Snyder.

Dedication

God waits for his temple to be built of love
While his people bring stones.

—TAGORE

God knows my worldly wealth is counted in pebbles, not stones, and so, with love, I offer this little book of confidences.

Also with love, I dedicate it to my long-suffering husband and son. They have stuck by me through adventures, frustrations, and prayers for help, but when and if they read what I have said about them in this book, I fear they will strongly urge me to run away from home.

Contents

Introduction

> "The time has come," the Walrus said,
> "To talk of many things:
> Of shoes—and ships—and sealing wax—
> Of cabbages—and kings—
> And why the sea is boiling hot—
> And whether pigs have wings."
>
> FROM LEWIS CARROLL'S
> *THROUGH THE LOOKING GLASS*

The looking glass at my house—and perhaps at yours—sometimes shows cabbages and pork chops and sometimes even kings and wings. So maybe you will not wonder why I put God in the same phrase with graham crackers and galoshes. Maybe you will understand that when I've had a crumby or drippy day, God has helped me find chuckles in the crumbs and delights in the downpours.

My friends and fellow sufferers tell me they have had similar experiences with the toils and tickles of every day, so I have looked through my memory bank and written down "talk of many things" that have happened through the years. I hope my meanderings will give you a smile and a prayer.

When the writer, Eudora Welty, was asked about her stories and her reasons for writing, she mentioned "the impulse to praise, to love, to call up, to prophesy." God knows I have no talent for prophesying, but maybe the little stories in this book will remind you to call up your own everyday happenings and help you find in them love and praise.

As Tagore writes, "Faith is the bird that feels the light / And sings / When the dawn is still dark." And so, I thank all my family and friends—and readers—who have listened to my singing. And I thank God who gave me the song.

—*Bernadette McCarver Snyder*

Graham Crackers and Galoshes

raham crackers and galoshes may be God's greatest gift to woman, but what KIND of woman? Can you imagine a Hollywood beauty queen on her knees trying to stuff galoshes onto a six-year-old who is wearing a snowsuit, sweater, mittens, ski mask, and two pairs of socks? Only a sausage stuffer could identify with that. The beautiful people would never understand.

Graham crackers may be a great gift because they can be used as pacifiers for all ages, and they are also the foundation and roof of "s'mores," those calorie-laden goodies made by sticking a marshmallow and chocolate bar between graham crackers and toasting until this creation is melted enough to permanently glue your teeth and intestines together in terminal sugar overload.

But what about the elusive graham-cracker leftover—the crumb trail? Can you imagine the president of a national corporation having the stamina to search out graham cracker crumbs from behind sofa cushions, underneath that ten-thousand-pound refrigerator, between the pages of school-books, or out of the furry linings of little bunny slippers?

And that's the easy part. The CHALLENGE comes when you MISS a few crumbs that little fingers have managed to mix with milk, cherry soda, or hot chocolate, and you don't find them until a week later, when the crumbs have turned to cement and are lurking on the underside of your kitchen table. Let the biochemists and nuclear scientists tackle THAT problem a few times!

It is psychologically unwise for me to thumb through fashion magazines, looking at slim, smiling models wearing this year's "latest" while I ponder my fingernails broken on snow-boot zippers, and my spirit broken by the graham-cracker cover-up. Did I really spend all those years reading the right books and improving my right brain so I could become chairperson of the graham-crackers-and-galoshes conglomerate?

———◦§◦———

Dear Lord, forgive my grass-is-greener complex. I KNOW my job is important. I KNOW this too shall pass and we shall move from galoshes to greener pastures. I even know that someday I will look back fondly and remember how wonderful it was "way back then." But don't let me waste today waiting for tomorrow.

Help me take advantage of the joys of HERE and NOW. Thank you, Lord, for designing those tiny fingers just right to hold a graham cracker. Thank you for letting me see that funny frown of determination as that little foot tries valiantly to push itself into the wiggly galosh. Thank you, Lord, for giving me someone to care for, to clean up after, and to get hugs and giggles from.

Remind me, Lord, that those "beautiful people" with the perfect nails might have a job just as frustrating as mine, one

without the fringe benefits of sunny backyard lunches and romps in the park, "discovering" butterflies and blades of grass and snails and shiny rocks, and cozy storytelling at bedtime followed by "I wuv you, Mommy."

Help me remember that the graham-crackers-and-galoshes routine isn't "all there is" to your wonderful world, but remind me that even if it were, it would be enough.

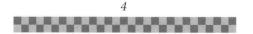

What's That Nonsterile Tomato-Plant Stake Doing in a Hospital?

Have you ever noticed that the parents who make their kids wear raincoats are always the ones you see in hospital emergency rooms? Parents who tell their kids to go play in traffic NEVER have emergencies. Their kids are indestructible.

But the Nervous Nellies and Watchful Willies, whose vocabularies are stuffed with WATCH OUT, BE CAREFUL, DON'T, and NEVER, NEVER, have kids who are allergic to air, can choke on a single strand of spaghetti, and break bones in a strong wind.

My kid has had two broken bones. The first one got broken when I took him with me to a PRAYER GROUP so he wouldn't have to stay home alone and get hurt. The second was when I was watching out the kitchen window so nothing would happen to him.

That second break is etched in my memory. The minute his shrieks of "MY ARM IS BROKEN" filled the neighborhood like an air-raid siren, two Boy Scouts appeared as if by magic. They announced that they had taken first-aid courses and would now splint his arm.

Evidently they believed in improvisation. My neighbor's garden patch was handy, so they quickly snatched up two tall sticks that had been the sole support of some hearty tomato plants. They slapped those muddy sticks on my son's arm and tied the whole thing together with an old handkerchief. Now we were ready to leave for the hospital.

At that time our budget was very small and so was our car. Can you imagine trying to get a whimpering kid with tomato-plant stakes tied to his arm into a Volkswagen bug? The trip on the highway was almost as funny as the look on the doctor's face when he saw our nonsterile splints.

But the arm healed perfectly, and after that, I told the kid to go play in traffic so he would be safe.

—⁓ఁ⁓—

Dear God, thank you for the emergencies that make me turn to you and trust in you. Help me to take care of the things I can, but count on you to take care of the things I can't. Help me to be cautious but not paranoid, trusting but not gullible, adventurous but not foolhardy, alert but not frenetic.

And, Lord, if you manage to make me all those things, then send me to the United Nations so I can spread it around!

An Electrifying Problem

My husband has seen the light. And he hated it.

He has seen the light burning bright in the basement because I forgot to turn it off. He has seen the light left on in the laundry room. The light shining all night in the garage. The light on the patio, on the front porch, in the bathroom, and even that little light in the oven. He didn't like what he saw.

My husband is afraid of the light more than other people are afraid of the dark. Even on a storm-tossed night, he does not believe in leaving a light burning in the window.

All I ever hear from him is: "Did you remember to turn off the light on the stairs? Be sure all the lights are off when you leave the house. Did you know there's a light left on in the bedroom? Why didn't you turn off the kitchen light?" This nonalternating current is about to make me blow a fuse!

One day I read an article about how few pennies it costs to pay for lights left on, and I tried to shed a little light on the situation by offering to give my husband some pennies. He

didn't think that was funny—or even a bright idea. I thought about offering to save my mad money and pay the electric bill every month, but I knew that would ruin all his fun. He'd have to find a new hobby! In fact, I'll bet right now he is saving up HIS mad money to buy me a lovely gift that I can take with me wherever I go—one of those flashlights that fits onto your belt.

⁓৯⁓

ear Lord, could you send a flash of heavenly light and tell my husband that there are more important problems on the planet, and even in our household, than whether or not I have turned off all the lights? I know that this is important to him for some strange reason (other than the light bill—which isn't high), and I have TRIED to pretend that I share his concern, but I just can't seem to program myself for the darkness. Please help me to be more careful or help him to be more tolerant.

Or maybe you could just point out to him that passage in Genesis: "God made the light—and saw that it was GOOD."

Impossible Dreams

I have been known to dream about red sports cars, trips to Hawaii, finding a brown bag with a million dollars in it, and hot-fudge sundaes. But last week, suddenly my wildest dreams focused on one of the few things still known to exist that is neither illegal, immoral, nor fattening—LETTUCE.

As a lifelong dieter, lettuce had never been on my list of passionate desires, UNTIL I went to the grocery and saw the price had suddenly jumped from 99 cents to $1.99. The farmers must have had a crop nipped in the bud or the grocer must have become money-mad. But there it was, plain old it-isn't-easy-being-green lettuce—suddenly a forbidden fruit.

As a protest, I left it at the grocery store, along with the steak, lobster, and other expensive no-nos. BUT on the way home, at night watching television, in the morning driving in the carpool, and in most of my waking moments, all I could think of was LETTUCE!

Suddenly I craved tacos topped with mounds of shredded lettuce, BLT sandwiches, a mystery dip made almost entirely of

lettuce (a recipe I had made only once and never planned to make again), and even low-calorie lettuce salad.

At $1.99 for a small head, lettuce had suddenly become a luxury, a gourmet collector's item, and one of the things I wanted to be stranded with on a desert island!

---

ear Lord, isn't it strange how we take things for granted until they become scarce? Water is a throwaway until the pipes freeze or the sewer gets clogged and you have to turn off the water until the repairs are finished. Air is always there until it gets polluted. Family members are the ones who turn up the television too loud and leave books, shoes, and newspapers in the middle of every room UNTIL the husband is out of town and the son is spending a night with a friend and you suddenly realize how tidy and quiet the house is. And how lonely. Dear Lord, help me to see your blessings before I lose them.

Thank you for the extraordinary ordinary bits of my life—the crazy friends who tell crazy jokes, that first cup of coffee and that last good-night kiss, the way the morning sun shines in my kitchen window and the all-day son comes in full of stories from school and new ideas and a case of the hungries.

Thank you for a warm coat and a warm blanket and warm oatmeal with brown sugar and warm handshakes and hellos.

And thank you, Lord, for listening, even when the subject is as silly as lettuce.

I'm Not Number One

'm #515-02010-6937 and #414-650-3916. I'm a Social Security number, a telephone number, a MasterCharge number, but NOT a hot number.

No one cares about my name, my needs, my nerves, my no-nos, only my numbers. Where will it all end? Numbers are programmed to go into infinity. I am not. I can hardly make it to ten p.m.

Somewhere, someone convinced us that numbers would be our salvation. Call a number and you will immediately receive your piece of the rock. Call a number and an embarrassingly rich Joe's pizza will miraculously appear at your door, dripping cheese on your carpet. Call a number and make an appointment and your new hairdo will transform you into a television model. Call a number and give them your number and charge your way into infinity and bankruptcy.

I think someone sure did a number on us.

Dear Lord, I am MORE than a number. I am an individual, a one-of-a-kind model, an exclusive design, a never-before and never-again original. You know that. And I know that.

Maybe that's all that matters. I want OTHERS to know that I'm unique, but maybe I'm spending more on the struggle than it's worth. Maybe I should relax in your love for a while. Bask in the knowledge that YOU know I'm special. Revel in the quirks and nuances and idiosyncrasies that are mine alone. They may be a little weird, but they're mine.

Thank you, Lord, for making me ME. Today I'm going to enjoy it. Maybe tomorrow I'll start trying to prove or improve it.

OOPS

When you are in the midst of child rearing, you can find oodles of books and articles that openly discuss your most private problems—burping, diaper rash, pacifier dependency, colic, temper tantrums, spinach spoon-feeding, and *mater dementia* (Mommy's hysteria). The only two questions I have not seen answered in print are: "If Susie sucks her thumb every day except Thursday, is that a Freudian clue that she will grow up to be a pediatrician or an orthodontist?" and "When Johnny hides in his closet with a bowl of spaghetti and makes designs with it all over the closet floor, does this mean he will grow up to be a famous Italian chef or will he someday learn to tie his shoelaces?"

A friend called me one day with wonderful news. "I just read this great article," she said. "It lists all the things you absolutely MUST teach your child before he is eighteen months old or it will be too late. There's only one problem—MY kid is nineteen months old today."

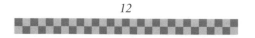

I could empathize with her. I read "Sixteen Foolproof Ways to Fool Your Child Into Throwing Away the Pacifier" the day after my son went into pacifier withdrawal. It started when he was leaning over a sewer pipe (he was always interested in such sanitary cultural objects). There was a grill on top of the pipe, but lucky for me there was a hole in the grill.

The kid was so fascinated by the sewer that he momentarily let go of the plug in his mouth (which he affectionately referred to as his "Chew Chew") and it fell through the hole in the sewer grill. Even at that age, my son was smart enough to know that Mommy was too fat to crawl into the sewer opening to get it for him, and Chew Chew was gone forever.

Next I read "Prerequisites for Preschool Parenting" the day he started first grade, and "Elementary and Essential Tips for Mothers of Elementary Grade Students" the day he started high school.

I fully expect to discover articles entitled "Puberty Previewed," "The Diary of a Happy Adolescent," and "You Can Still Be a Hit With Zits" the day after he gets married.

———⌒§⌒———

Dear God, so often life seems to happen one day too late. Help me to survive in spite of all the missed opportunities. Help me to not cry over spilled milk or double-dip chocolate ice-cream sodas that I should have spilled instead of devoured. Help me to learn to leave the problems of yesterday in the hands of the historians and put the possible problems of tomorrow into your loving hands.

Lord, thank you for NOW. Help me to cherish it, savor it, LIVE it, and enjoy it—instead of waiting until it's a day too late.

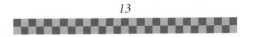

Saint Francis is for the Birds

When you see a picture of Saint Francis, the friend of animals, he always seems to be peacefully meditating and praying as he stands in a garden surrounded by lovely birds. Could he have been meditating about how to handle his house cat or survive his yard dog?

We have had one cat and one dog who were challenges to our patience, pocketbook, and devotion to Saint Francis.

Our yard dog was a combination of the Cookie Monster and Adolf Hitler. He was the best friend of every kid on the block, but he ruled me with total tyranny.

When he was with the kids, he ate what they ate—Popsicles, peanut-butter sandwiches, or even dry crackers. When I tried to get him to eat his nutritionally correct dog food, he would fast for days until, in desperation, I smothered it in bacon grease and fed it to him by hand.

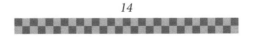

He would escape from our fenced yard with the ease of Houdini and would visit every neighbor who had no desire to be visited. Although we lavished him with love, doggie treats, and a dog house with wall-to-wall carpeting, he regularly ran away from home. When he returned, covered with mud, brambles, and unknown smelly substances, he would CRAWL across the front yard on his belly, wagging his tail and whimpering, in a bid to make the neighbors think that he only came back home because he had nowhere else to go.

I don't know why he had that split personality, but I always hoped it was the fault of his previous owners. We had adopted him when he was full-grown and "formerly owned." That's why my son always raised eyebrows by telling everyone we had a "used" dog.

Now we have a used cat. He started out as a furry, purry friend who liked to snuggle up in my lap and sit on my son's shoulder while he did homework. But the cat soon developed into another "challenge," one who was faster than a speeding mother, more powerful than a pleading boy, and able to leap tall sofas in a single bound.

Some of our friends had an "alleluia" cat. He got loose on a trip to the vet and ran away. They searched for hours, but finally had to go home cat-less. Weeks later, the night before Easter, they had reason to shout alleluia when he suddenly turned up at their back door—dirty, skinny, scarred from battle, weary from the journey, but resurrected.

Our cat does not know how close he has come to NEEDING a resurrection. He lies in wait behind a corner and "ambushes" us as we come into a room. A surprise attack like that could easily lead to his losing at least one of his nine lives.

He has become addicted to a certain piece of rope with a knot tied in the end. He expects us to drag it across the floor for him to chase at least twelve hours out of every twenty-four.

Otherwise, he meows mournfully and LOUDLY, thus endangering his species further.

He won't eat unless someone is sitting on the floor next to him, patting his head, and telling him what a wonderful cat he is. When you are ready to play with him, he isn't interested. When you are busy, he wants to play.

Both our used dog and cat seemed to know instinctively and immediately how to turn US into "used" owners.

Dear Lord, all the pets shown in magazines and on TV are always a real part of the family—cooperative, hardworking, loyal, and true. We showed our pets Lassie reruns and lots of magazine pictures, but it didn't do a bit of good.

When Saint Francis spoke, the animals LISTENED. Maybe that's because they sensed his inner peace. Our animals must have sensed our inner panic.

Dear Lord, we're always in such a hurry. We don't have TIME to chase a piece of rope across the floor or sit and bask in your sunshine and blessings. Help me to learn from that, Lord. Help me to take the time to bask.

You know, Lord, our pets are completely dependent on us, but they are too independent to realize it. Help me to learn from that too, Lord. I am completely dependent on you, but sometimes I am too busy doing my own thing to realize it.

Forgive my hardheaded determination to do things MY way instead of your way. Help me to accept, Lord. Help me to trust. Give me the faith to follow where you lead.

And, Lord, would you please tell Saint Francis there is a delinquent cat living at our house who could use a good talking-to from someone who speaks his language.

Guilty or Not Guilty?

Guilt sure can give you tired blood! Today, as I view my kingdom...or is that queendom...or persondom?...ahem...today, as I look around this dump, I see a guilt trip waiting to strike. The grass is as high as an elephant's eye; there is laundry waiting to be done; the refrigerator has a musty smell, so I know it's time for a search-and-destroy mission; if I don't get my hair washed in the next ten minutes, terminal greasiness will set in; and I just ran out of bread and milk.

Boy, am I tired, thinking about all that!

And the worst part is that if I manage to get all those emergencies handled by suppertime, an equal number of new ones will crop up by the time I get the supper dishes done.

Every criminal has at least a chance of hearing "not guilty" when the verdict is handed down, but every housewife knows that she hasn't got a chance! No matter how much she accomplishes, at the end of the day, there's still going to be a little undone chore somewhere, just waiting to jump out from behind something and smirk "GUILTY!"

No wonder we have tired blood, tired hair, tired excuses, and a very tiring habit of whining a lot.

~§~

ear Lord, thank you for all my little chores, they keep me so humble! But Lord, eating humble pie every day can be boring, fattening, and bad for my physical and mental health. Help me to get off this guilt trip and into some kind of class on "time management techniques"!

I realize that no matter how much I do or how well I do it, I will NEVER get it all done. So, Lord, just help me to face my limitations, to do as much as I can every day to be dutiful and still save some time for you, for me, for the family, and for exploring new horizons. In other words, Lord, let's get this guiltdom ORGANIZED!

Weather or Not

'M HOMESICK. For the past few weeks we've had a stroke of bad weather—snow, ice, impassable roads, and impossible temperatures. So the weather has made me stay home whether I wanted to or not. It was just what I had dreamed of: an excuse for not running errands or attending meetings or going anywhere, a chance to stay by the fire and get all my long overdue chores done. Well, it was wonderful at first, but now I'm beginning to go stir crazy and get home "sick."

I've cleaned out closets, cleaned the floors, cleaned the kitchen pantry, and cleaned out the kitchen refrigerator (by eating everything in there)! Now my house looks clean, I look fat, and I'm so home "sick" I could die.

And the worst part is that there are still lots of chores on my list, waiting to be done; but, instead of doing them, all I can think about is how much fun it would be to go somewhere. I actually think it would be fun to go grocery shopping, go to the drugstore, to the shoe-repair store, or even to the plumbing supply store—just GO anywhere.

Well, if it doesn't stop snowing soon, I will. I'll go bananas, berserk, or back to the refrigerator!

———※———

Dear Lord, surely you have some control over this weather! Couldn't you give us a break before I have a breakdown? Oh, I know, I know; it's not YOUR fault, it's mine. When I was running around like a merry-go-round, always on the go, but never getting anywhere, I yearned for the quiet of home and hearth. But now that I've had a nice, refreshing dose of "H and H," I can't wait to get back on the go. I'm never satisfied. The grass is always greener. Forgive me, Lord, for my unsatisfiability.

Teach me to be content with, and grateful for, what I have, where I am, who I am, and why I am.

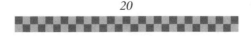

That Terrible Craving

Here it is the middle of winter, with snow all over the highways and the alleys, the movie marquees and the manholes—and yet I have this crass craving, this larcenous longing, this dumb desire, to go to a garage sale.

I KNOW that I have to wait for the green buds of springtime to remind housewives of the greenbacks they can make by selling their trash-and-treasures. I KNOW that I have to wait for the warm spring/summer breezes that will tantalizingly wave the corner signs made with crayons and colored markers on the backs of old pieces of cardboard—the signs that say Yard Sale, BIG BARGAINS, Moving Sale, Lots of Loot (and other such tauntingly seductive phrases). I KNOW that I have to wait, and yet I yearn.

I long for the satisfaction of snatching up a bargain before someone else spots it, for the glee of grabbing up a choice item JUST as the lady in the bandanna was reaching for it.

I hunger for the thrill of dashing into a strange garage with a few dollar bills and some change, and staggering out, arms loaded down with bargains and boodle. (It's so much more

fun than staggering into a grocery store loaded down with cash, and dashing out with a few dollar buns and some hamburger.)

Ah, for those crazy, hazy, lazy days—those days of signs and poses. Following the signs, then posing and pretending that I absolutely will NOT buy a bauble or bangle unless the seller knocks off a nickel here, a dime there. Arriving home in the sluggish afternoon, clutching my treasures. Washing them (and finding the chip I didn't notice), polishing them (and discovering the black spot ISN'T tarnish that will polish away but just a black spot), placing them in those "certain spots" where they just fit and will be sure to become favorite conversation pieces.

I sigh and look about me at last year's acquisitions—the silver bowl that didn't polish up good enough to grace the dining table but looks elegant with my English ivy growing out of it, the only-slightly-unbalanced coatrack that stands up straight and handsome since I wedged it in the hall corner, the old washday boiler painted black that was just right to hold logs next to the fireplace.

Yes, I know. It's a MADNESS, a craving. I should kick the habit and give up garages. But even now, in the clean white snow of winter, I long for a dark dirty garage with a SALE sign on it!

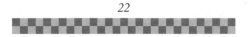

Dear Lord, why do we always yearn for MORE? My house is full of ten-cent treasures, so why do I have the itchy-finger virus, always looking for MORE? My closet is full of clothes (some that fit, some that don't), so why do I always think one more outfit might make me look ten pounds thinner? Forgive my love of shopping, my need to change things around, my plotting and planning to do something DIFFERENT. Maybe it's a sign, Lord, of my yearning for YOU. In always searching, maybe it is you I am searching for. My need to change the house may be a symbol of my inner need to change myself. My need to add to my possessions may be a result of my need to possess YOU more. Help me sort out my priorities, Lord. Help me empty my life a bit, so I will have more time for prayer and more room to be filled by thoughts of you.

But forgive me, Lord, if my car automatically turns in at a garage sale once in a while. Woman does not live by prayer alone.

Opposites Attract— Trouble!

W hy is it that a fair damsel who prefers to sleep until noon except in cases of national emergency always seems to marry a handsome devil who is convinced that a tree falling in the forest will make no sound if there is no one there to hear and a sun rising will shed no light unless HE is there to see!

Why is it that a female who loves the theater, classical music, and sometimes the ballet marries a male who thinks a "symphonic movement" is the passage of a two-hundred-pound hulk as he moves a small brown ball from one end of a football field to another?

When the honeymoon is over, you will observe the damsel struggling to face the dawn even though she knows her blood will not start circulating until noon. You will notice the husband wedged into a theater seat with his eyes fixed on the stage in rapt attention, as he listens to a game with the radio earphones wedged into his ear.

Why is human nature so perverse? A computer would never make two such unlike hearts beat as one.

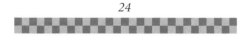

But as long as humans keep getting married without the help of computers, that opposites-attract syndrome will continue to plague modern civilization and to threaten domestic bliss. I know. I speak from experience.

I like lilting dance music. My husband thinks it's monotonous. He likes Civil War history. I think it's boring. I like going places, doing things. He likes staying home by the fire. I like exotic foods. He likes steak and potatoes. But I like him. And he likes me.

Dear God, thank you for making me learn firsthand that I can love and be loved by someone who does not think or act or LIKE as I do. Help me to remember this when I deal with the world, when I encounter people at church or on a committee or at work or at a party who do not look at the world the same way I do. Before I condemn them because of our differences, let me see them as you do.

I'm not asking you to let me be a marshmallow with no opinions. I couldn't stand that and neither could you. Just help me to bend enough to TRY to comprehend others' ideas and preferences.

And as for my opposite but wonderful husband, Lord, remind me to not be so grouchy at dawn and help me to remove that pained, long-suffering look from my face when I am ENDURING one of his "likes." And oh, yes, Lord, could you please inspire the FCC to make a sudden irreversible ruling that will outlaw either Sunday afternoon or Monday night football games? Two days in a row is too much—even for a likable person like me!

What Can You Expect of a Day That Starts With Dirty Dishes?

oes dried-up egg yolk on a plate remind you of sunshine? Does baked-on gravy make you feel like a little kid wiggling your toes on a muddy riverbank? If you answered yes, seek professional help immediately. You are definitely running off the beaten path.

For many of us across the land, the dawn does not come up like thunder. It comes up with the rattle of dirty dishes. No matter how late you stay up sanitizing the kitchen at night, the next morning there will be DIRTY DISHES somewhere. Either they regenerate

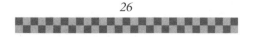

themselves, or somebody up there wants me to have dishpan hands.

If God had meant me to spend my life at the sink, wouldn't he have made my pinkie a dishmop and my thumb a scouring pad? Surely God had bigger things in mind for me than scraping and scrubbing gravy spots (especially when I know I should have been eating Melba toast instead of gravy!). Did God REALLY give me the dirty-dish syndrome because he loves me???

Dear God, help me to remember to be thankful that we have such an abundance of food that we can afford to have so many dirty dishes. Help me to see the SON shine of Jesus' love in the egg yolk left on the plates of people who love me. Make me realize how lonely it would be to have only Melba-toast-clean plates and no peanut-butter fingerprints or Kool-Aid kisses.

Dear God, thank you for my dirty dishes.

But don't be surprised if I forget and complain again tomorrow.

The Great
Equalizer

Women who picket and protest may think THEY were responsible for forcing men to empathize with the trials and tribulations of women. Actually, it was the BLOW-DRYER.

For years, women suffered alone, UNTIL, upon the horizon loomed HAIR STYLING for men. The Great Equalizer had come.

At last men could understand the heartbreak of psoriasis is nothing compared to the heartbreak of a hairdo that won't do. Now they realized even acne or BAD BREATH pale beside the trauma of a tress undressed, a wave gone wrong, or a curl that won't.

After years of being free, footloose, and unfettered, those poor men gave up crewcuts and that greasy kid stuff to become slaves to the permanent wave, the conditioners, setting gels, sprays, rinses, and tints. John Wayne look-alikes laid down their six-guns and picked up their blow-dryers.

Didn't men have ENOUGH trouble trying to be breadwinners and war winners, macho yet gentle, assertive yet understanding, and able to make touchdowns in a single bound? Now they know what real trouble is.

I can still remember my high school prom, looking in the mirror and knowing that I had just the right dress, just the right shoes, and just the wrong hair.

When I think of my wedding, I remember how handsome the groom looked, how pretty the flowers were, how happy I was, and how it took forty-seven coats of hair spray to make that one curl turn IN instead of out.

Now men will share such memories. The big football game, and you get the frizzies. An interview for an executive position, and your extrastrong superhold hair spray doesn't. The night of the father-son banquet and the high school neighborhood has a power blackout because the men and the boys all rev up their blow-dryers at the same time.

It was an ill wind that blew blow dryers into the men's room.

—⟨§⟩—

Dear God, equality is wonderful, isn't it? Misery loves company. But I know I'm not supposed to laugh. I'm supposed to empathize.

Please help us ALL—hes and shes—to remember the "lilies of the field" and worry more about what's IN the head instead of what's on it or around it. Help us to be less concerned with the fashion of the day and more concerned with the promise of eternity. Fill our heads with the glory of your love so we won't care if our "crowning glory" isn't.

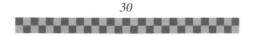

Do Old Wives Really Tell Tales?

W hy is it we always hear about old wives' tales? It seems to me that old husbands are the ones who tell tall tales!

And yet, all the ancient advice and sage superstitions are labeled as having come from old wives. I never thought of my mother as an old wife because, even in her seventies, she seemed so young—but she did have an O.W.T. to fit every situation.

She was firmly convinced that warts could be cured by wiping them with an old dishcloth and then burying the cloth in the backyard! And if you walked under a ladder, you would have bad luck. But if you ate carrots, you would have good eyesight and if you ate rhubarb, you would have rosy cheeks! (Every time she served rhubarb, she would say, "Look what we're having today—rosy cheeks!")

I'm not sure all of those classify as old wives' tales, but we were careful to eat our carrots and rhubarb, never walk under a ladder, and keep an old dishcloth on hand at all times just in case a wart might pop up.

And now, every springtime when the sun is "hot enough to

fry an egg on the sidewalk" (another of Mother's expressions) and I am enjoying the sunshine on the patio and thinking about putting away my winter clothes, I remember to keep out a sweater because the snowball bush hasn't bloomed yet.

Mother always told me that as soon as our snowball bush bloomed, the weather would turn snowy-cold again for a few days. I never believed her, and went right ahead and got out the shorts and swimsuit and stored away the wintry woolens. And then, one morning we'd wake up and discover that, suddenly, the temperature was sending chills up our spines and everywhere else and I had to frantically search out a sweater and warm slacks. And, as I was dashing off late for school, I would notice that the bush by the porch was in full bloom— the snowballs had sent us to the mothballs for winter clothes again!

This morning, as I stood by my kitchen sink, looking out the window at my own snowball bush covered with those big, white, fluffy blossoms, I snuggled into my sweater and sipped my hot tea and smiled nostalgically, thinking, "Mother's right, again!"

~⊸§⊸~

ﮙear Lord, why is that children of all ages find it so hard to give mothers credit for being "right"? I guess it's the idea that if Mother is "always right" that somehow implies that WE must always be wrong. Forgive us, Lord. Remind your children to honor their mothers and to say, "You're right, Mom" and "Thanks, Mom" and "I love you, Mom" before it's too late.

But, Lord, when the archaeologists of the future start looking for clues to our civilization, what are they going to think about all those dishcloths buried in backyards?

I Deserve a Break Today

I need a break. But I'm afraid to pray for it.

One of my friends prayed for a break, and the next week she fell down and broke her leg! That wasn't exactly the kind of break she had in mind!

It makes me wonder if maybe God, like our children, only listens to HALF of what we say! No, no, I know that's not true. He listens all right, and always answers. It's just that sometimes his interpretation is not the same as mine. I ask for a hot-fudge sundae and he hands me a pickle. Well, that's okay. I like pickles, but it just wasn't what I was expecting.

Actually, God's "interpretations" used to make me really mad until I finally realized that he sends me what I need instead of what I ask for. And it always works out okay—even my friend's broken leg. At least she got to put her feet up for a while and didn't have to wash dishes!

But I think maybe I'm going to try something different today. I'm going to pray for a pickle—and see if God will send me a hot-fudge sundae!

Dear Lord, I hope you weren't listening to all that. I was just kidding. I know you can surprise me, but I can't surprise you. And I know you pay attention to prayers, just not to instructions. Besides, I'd be in a lot of trouble if you had given me some of the things I've prayed for through the years. And so many times you have given me something so much better than what I asked for. I asked for cabbage and you sent me creamy coleslaw. I asked for just a little light and you sent Roman candles. Thank you, Lord, for sending me so many sweet surprises.

Hi, Neighbor

There was a certain neighborhood that I occasionally drove through, going to a garage sale, leaving the scene of a Boy Scout picnic, or taking an emergency route to a dollar-day sale. I didn't like that neighborhood. There was no specific reason. I just didn't like it.

A few years ago when our first house became unfriendly because its walls were bulging, we decided to look for one a little larger. One of the first things I told the real-estate agent was not to look in that neighborhood.

I soon found that house-hunting is not as much fun as house tours. It is about as much fun as trying on clothes after you have been to nine Christmas brunches, lunches, and all-you-can-eat buffets. The houses didn't fit. They were too little or too dull or too expensive or too-too.

One day my real-estate friend called and said she had FOUND SOMETHING. We dashed out to see it. She was right. It was the right size, price, and neighborhood. But it didn't "feel" right. It didn't say hello. This was not easy to explain to her OR to myself.

By now she was getting desperate, having spent a lot of time and gasoline on my quest. She said, "Look, there's one other

house that has everything you want, dining room, double garage, and so on, but it's in the neighborhood you don't like. Since we're out anyway, let's just take a look at it." Grudgingly, I agreed.

When we drove up to it, I knew it was MINE. The minute we stepped in the door, everything was "me"—the colors, the carpets, the drapes, the room layout, the view, AND the price. When my husband saw it, he agreed. We signed the contract that day.

The neighborhood turned out to be perfect: the people were wonderful; it was convenient to church, school, all my favorite places to shop; and it was five minutes, through a back way, to the highway my husband took to work.

Later that summer, as I sat on my new front porch looking out at the kind of view I had dreamed of, I realized that sometimes I judge people the same way I had misjudged that neighborhood. I don't like them because I don't know them, and I don't take time to take a second look. I could miss a lot of friends, and a lot opportunities, that way.

———

Dear Lord, help me to be slower to judge, more willing to look below the surface, before I decide something off the top of my head. Help me to remember Zacchaeus who was ridiculed, yet YOU chose him to visit, and Mary Magdalene who was scorned, but YOU chose her as a friend. Please, Lord, give me understanding, sympathy, and most of all, tolerance. And thank you, Lord, for MY neighborhood.

Dehumidified

This week our humidifier put me in a bad humor. In fact, it got me all steamed up!

My husband had mentioned that he didn't think it was working properly and asked if I would call and get it checked out. I called LAST WEEK to set up an appointment and asked that they make a note for the repair person to also clean the furnace on the same service call. The voice on the phone said that a service representative would be at our house at nine a.m. today. I said that would be fine but to be sure it was no later than nine a.m. because I had to leave the house at noon and I wanted to allow him plenty of time to work. I was assured that it would be absolutely no later than nine a.m.

At nine-forty-five a.m. today, when no one had arrived, I called to inquire. I was told that he was on his way. At ten-forty-five a.m. today, I called again and said they should just forget sending him because it was too late now for him to have enough time to do anything. I also told them that I would call another company which I hoped would be more reliable! At eleven-fifteen a.m. today, the serviceman arrived anyway. When

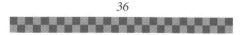

I questioned the time, he said no one had told him he was supposed to be here by nine a.m. and no one had told him that the call had been canceled.

I explained that I had to leave by noon, but he said that was no problem, he would have plenty of time to fix everything before then. He disappeared into the basement and began making noises. At eleven-forty-five a.m. today, he was still making noises and my time was running out. I went to the basement and he said he had taken the entire humidifier apart and could find nothing wrong with it, so he had put it back together just as before and he would be right up with the bill.

I stood in the doorway with coat on, purse under arm, and checkbook in hand, nervously tapping my foot. Finally, he came up the steps and presented me with a healthy bill for having left things just as they were when he arrived. Then he said, "Oh, by the  way, you should get someone to clean that furnace. It's pretty dirty." I said, "But YOU were supposed to clean the furnace." And he said, "I would have, but you said you had to leave at noon so I didn't have time."

I was so humidified I couldn't even argue with him. And I couldn't think fast enough to tell him I didn't have time to write the check either, but he needn't worry, I would get it to him by nine a.m. Monday or Thursday or absolutely no later than next year.

Instead, I just handed him the check, gritted my teeth, and headed for my appointment. I still can't believe it. How do

companies get away with service like that? Something similar happens almost every time I try to get anything fixed and it seems like the more I complain, the less good it does. Do you think I could sue for breach of promise?

—⌘—

ear Lord, what has happened to pride of workmanship? Doesn't anyone care anymore about a job well done, the "good name" of a company, the "good will" of a customer? I'm sure there must still be some efficient, "caring" companies out there somewhere so why can't I ever find one?

I'm sorry if I seem hard to please, Lord, but my friends tell me they have the same problem. Help us, Lord, to start turning this trend around. Help us FIRST to take pride in our OWN work, because we can't find fault in others if we are just as guilty. Then help us to teach our children to believe in the dignity of work and the responsibility to care enough to do your very best!

And, Lord, my furnace is still dirty and that humidifier is probably still not working, so do you think you could send an angel down to look at it? But please send one by nine p.m. because it will take time to do the job right, and I ABSOLUTELY have to get to sleep no later than midnight. And I don't think I could get to sleep while an angel was making noises in my basement!

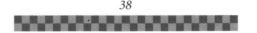

Do Fence Me In

In the movies, pioneer folks are always getting together for those barn raisings, and it looks like so much fun. You see men laughing and working, women baking and stirring and dishing up wonderful "vittles," and all rejoicing at the finished barn, joining in happy square dances and singing like the Mormon Tabernacle Choir.

We had a fence raising, and somehow it wasn't the same. Our patio had a nice little unambitious fence around it that was about to fall down, so we decided we had better see about getting a new one built. We did not plan to get emotionally or physically involved. We just planned to pay for it.

As it turned out, the price quoted was a lot more than we planned to pay. While we considered it, I happened to mention this fence of great price to my prayer group. I should have stuck to the praying. Two of the ladies immediately volunteered their husbands to raise our fence.

My husband was not thrilled with this turn of events. He is not your average everyday handyman, and he could not visualize it being fun like it is in the movies.

While we worried about imposing on our friends and how to avoid it, our friends went right ahead drawing up plans, ordering lumber, and setting up a work schedule.

The first day they came, they tore down the old fence and dug giant holes all over the yard for fence posts, and it really was fun. We had pizza and all the trimmings and laughed a lot. But before we realized it, the day was over and they were gone, along with our old fence, and we sat there looking at a very "holey" yard.

We spent a lot of time fretting about whether someone would fall in a hole and sue us or the neighborhood cat would jump in to satisfy his natural curiosity or the neighborhood toddler would fill in all the holes with his little toy shovel. None of it happened. The next weekend our friends showed up again, mixing concrete, putting in posts, laughing and joking. I felt compelled to top last week's pizza and cooked up a lunch fit for farm hands, and all was well.

Then the rains came. The mounds of dirt turned into pools of mud, the trench for a rerouted drain pipe became a raging torrent and the next workday had to be postponed.

Now I am the kind of person who would start on the Taj Mahal and expect it to be ready by Tuesday. Patience is not my most important product. When we had first discussed the fence

raising, our friends had talked about coming in the morning and finishing the fence by evening. That I could identify with. Building it a piece at a time, ONLY ON SATURDAY, was something to which I had to adjust.

But at last the final day dawned. It dawned cloudy, gray, with cold winds howling and a tornado watch! There was no rainbow or other sign in the sky; or if there was, it was too overcast for us to spot it.

I started stewing with worry while brewing a pot of chili and putting a big apple pie in the oven. And then it happened. The fence was finished! The storm clouds disappeared and the sun shone on a new fence that was twice as beautiful as we had expected and cost less than half what we had planned. I had worried about all the things that didn't happen. I had chewed fingernails for naught.

Dear Lord, help me to remember that you can see around the bends in the road and I can't. Help me to trust.

Forgive my anxiety about the "maybes" and the "what ifs."

Thank you for the friends who raise my spirits, as well as my fence. Help me to see the joy and exuberance of your creation in them and through them. Remind me to return the favor of your love.

Give me the fortitude to wait, the innocence to believe in small miracles, the courage to stop straining to see around the corner when I should just leave the looking and the driving to you.

But, Lord, if we ever need any further real-estate development at our house, remind me to discuss it carefully with you before I mention it to the prayer group.

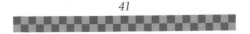

Born With a Silver (Tea) Spoon

All these years, I've been putting pudding, applesauce, cottage cheese, and so on, on my son's plate, accompanied by a TEASPOON. Today he said, "Please, Mother, I need a bigger spoon."

Does this mean that my little boy will soon be married with a family of his own—or just that he has a big mouth?

We mothers are never prepared for these important plateaus. We cry at the first day of kindergarten, the first bicycle, the first skateboard, the first skinned shin. Maybe that's how my face got all those wrinkles—from being WET all the time!

Mothers' tears sprinkle the first lost tooth, the first homemade valentine, the first Scout overnight, and the first pimple. And then, of course, mothers must cry at weddings. It's the good news and the bad news—the last great plateau for their kid but the THREAT of starting all over again with new plateaus for grandchildren!

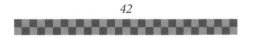

Dear God, forgive my fear of plateaus. When all is going smoothly, but THE SAME, I complain because it is BORING. Then as soon as a plateau appears, signaling some new phase of life, I'm scared to death. Help me see the new possibilities instead of just the new problems. Help me learn to climb the plateau—because it's there! (And if I get nosebleeds and varicose veins from all that climbing, remind me to thank you for letting me live in an age that has paper handkerchiefs and support stockings.)

Wanted: Letter From a Husband

The other day I was thumbing through an old book that pictured and told about some of the best magazine advertising from the past, and one ad really caught my eye. It was a Hamilton watch ad that must have appeared in a magazine at least forty years ago, and it pictured a pretty lady who was looking at her new Christmas watch and the note that came with it.

The note read, in part: "To Peggy, for marrying me in the first place, for bringing up our children while I mostly sat back and gave advice, for never getting sore at my always getting sore at your bridge playing, for planning a thousand meals a year and having them taken for granted, for a constant tenderness I rarely notice but am sure I couldn't live without, for just being you, Darling, here's your Hamilton watch with all my love."

I was "stricken" by that ad because last Christmas my husband gave me a watch. Instead of writing me a note, he said one morning in December, "Why don't you go out and pick out whatever kind of watch you'd like and put it under the Christmas tree, from me." Isn't that romantic?

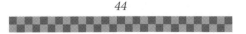

Maybe he's just lazy or maybe he's influenced by TODAY'S kind of advertising. An ad for a gift for a woman today usually shows the woman dashing off in the morning, wearing designer clothes and carrying a Gucci briefcase, on the way to her executive office. Next, we see her jetting to London for a business lunch, then jetting back and stopping on her way from the airport to pick up a few groceries. Back at home, she emerges in another dressier designer outfit, ready to dance the night away. Who would dare write a mushy, sentimental love letter to a superwoman like that? She might correct the punctuation.

Of course, most of us aren't superwomen except in our daydreams. And you know, I bet if most husbands really sat down to write a letter to their wives today, it would sound pretty much like the note in that old ad.

Along with the old ad I found, there was the story behind the ad. The man who had written it said that he had decided to just sit down and write an ad as if he were writing to his own wife, and that's what he came up with. He also noted that after the ad appeared, his company received hundreds of letters from men saying things like, "I am copying your ad word for word to include with my Christmas present for my wife. You have put into words what I have long thought but have never been able to say."

After I read that, my feelings weren't hurt at all by last year's Christmas watch, handpicked by me. I knew that if my husband had to sit down, like the advertising writer, and write me a note, he would have said all those things and more. And I also remembered that MY Christmas present to him didn't include even a gift card, much less a note.

So next year I think I'm going to suggest that we forget presents and just write each other a Christmas letter!

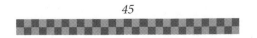

Dear Lord, thank you for all the things that we don't HAVE to say to each other anymore, because we know they're true. But you know, woman does not live by truth alone. She also needs some hearts and flowers now and then. And maybe man does too. Help us to remember not to take each other for granted, Lord, to take the time to tell each other how we feel and think and love. And forgive us, Lord, for sometimes taking YOU for granted too, neglecting to offer up to you our love and feelings and thoughts. And thank you, Lord, for gifting us with the hearts and flowers.

From Trash to Treasure?

f today was a fish, I'd throw it back in! This morning I went out and discovered that during the night somebody's dog had knocked over our garbage can, strewing our trash across the yard for all to see (I had to re-can it), and somebody's car had knocked over our mailbox (I will have to get it re-posted).

I came in to console myself with a cup of coffee, but as I turned to carry the coffee to the table, my arm hit the counter and coffee spilled all over my newly mopped floor (I had to re-mop). It now seemed indicated to console myself still more so I looked around for a forbidden snack, but the cupboard was bare (I will have to get to the grocery store and re-stock).

While I was out trashing the garbage can, I must have picked up a snootful of the pollen that evidently hangs heavy today because my nose started a nonstop sneezing spree. It has now been blown and re-blown until I think I will also have to be re-nosed.

When the sneezes finally slowed, I started my usual fifty-yard dash through the house. This is my daily hide-and-seek-and-ye-shall-never-find-again pickup, cleanup, put-away, pitch-away mission impossible. It did not go well. I dropped the button I was supposed to sew on my husband's shirt and it fell

into the bathroom sink and disappeared down the drain. I tore the corner of the fitted sheet, and can't fix it because the only thing I know how to sew is buttons. And I accidentally closed up the cat in the closet. Now I need to re-button, re-sheet, and re-cat.

There is definitely something fishy about this day. Should I try to regroup and recoup? Or just give up and resign and recline?

⟶◦§◦⟵

Dear Lord, why is it that some days get off to a bad start and never stop? I would think it's my fault (as usual); but I'm not anymore disorganized today than I was yesterday, and yesterday went fine. Oh, oh, Lord, I just realized what happened.

Do you remember yesterday, Lord? The minute I woke up, a thought popped into my head, and this was most unusual since usually NOTHING can get through the fog in my head for at least two hours. That's how I knew YOU had put the thought there. And the thought was, "This is the day the Lord has made. Let us rejoice and be glad."

All during the day, whenever anything went amiss, those words would come back to me and I would get glad again. By the end of the day, I had resolved that I would remember to start EVERY day with those words, so of course, today, on the very first day afterward, I forgot to remember! Forgive me, Lord.

Even on a day that starts with trash, pollen, lost buttons, and a closet-encased kitty cat, I am most richly blessed. In fact, if I started counting my blessings, I wouldn't know how to count that high. Thank you, Lord, thank you. And I promise I will remember every morning from now on to say those beautiful words, "This is the day the Lord has made. Let us rejoice and be glad."

But just in case I ever forget, Lord, please re-mind me.

Going With the Green Light

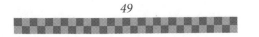

o you realize that probably the greatest sign of faith in the world today is that little green left-turn arrow on stoplights?

We are always reading statistics and surveys about how nobody has faith in anything anymore. They tell us that no one believes in the American flag, motherhood, or apple pie. No one believes in the family or in religion or morality. No one believes in the past, the present, or the future. So why does everyone believe in that little green arrow?

Here you and your car sit at a red light, waiting. Ahead, on the other side of the street, you can see rows and rows of cars coming straight toward you. You know if even one of those cars smashed into you, it could dramatically change your present AND your future. But the minute that little green arrow lights up, your foot is on the pedal and you GO. You turn left, right across the path of those oncoming blobs of metal, exposing your broadside and TRUSTING that everyone will follow the rules and stop before hitting you.

Why is that? Why do we trust a little green arrow more than

the American flag, motherhood, and apple pie? Does this mean that all we have to do to get back our national pride is to exchange our stars and stripes for little green arrows?

~§~

Dear Lord, forgive us for trusting a traffic signal more than we trust you. Every day you give us signals and directions much more important than that little green arrow, but we of little faith are afraid to follow YOUR signs. Instead of putting our foot on the pedal to go, we hesitate, we wonder, we doubt.

It's hard, Lord. Today there are so many signs blinking at us from all directions. It's hard to know which ones to follow, hard to know which ones are REALLY yours. Help us, Lord. Help us to know when to stop and when to go and which arrows point us in the way you want us to go.

And, Lord, don't worry, no matter what those surveys say, there are a lot of us who still believe in the American flag, motherhood, apple pie, AND YOU.

It Isn't Fair

W hy is it my cat never catches a cold? He sometimes catches field mice and often catches my attention, but although he seems to do everything in his power to catch a cold, he doesn't.

He goes out in the rain and gets his feet wet and never carries an umbrella. He wanders around in the wet grass and even stays out in the damp all night sometimes, but never even gets a sneeze or a sniffle.

In the wintertime, he even goes out in the snow BAREFOOT! He never wears galoshes or a warm scarf or a silly-looking wool hat. And poor kitten doesn't even have any mittens.

But poor me has mittens and scarves and several silly-looking wool hats, and what good does it do? While my cat is catching snowflakes on his nose and sloshing happily through every icy puddle, I am muffled up from head to toe and still catching every cold germ in the area. It isn't fair.

And in the summer while the cat is letting it rain on his parade and happily rolling in the wet grass, I am carefully keeping my feet dry, carrying an umbrella at all times (just in case), wearing a high-neck bathing suit, and catching cold germs right through my sunscreen. It isn't fair.

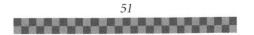

Of course, it isn't fair that some people live in mansions and I don't. And some people are big executives and I'm not. And some people take trips around the world and I don't. Oh, yes, I have been spending a lot of time recently making lists of all the haves and have-nots and isn't-fairs.

But the only problem is that when I do that, I finally have to admit that it also isn't fair that some people live in hovels and I don't. And some people are standing in line to try to get a bare subsistence unemployment check and I'm not. And some people have never traveled even a few miles from their home while I have been across the river and through the woods and even beyond.

And even though I catch colds, I don't have a chronic or life-threatening illness. And, although I'm not as rich as Rockefeller, as an American I have more material goods, freedoms, and opportunities than about ninety percent of the people in the world. In fact, I have to admit that there is really only ONE big thing that I am missing, one thing that could put sunshine in my psyche, one thing that could really change my world. And do you know what it is? An ATTITUDE OF GRATITUDE.

———

Dear Lord, I hate to admit it, but deep down I know that no matter how difficult the day, I can always look around and see someone who's having one that's worse. No matter how stressful the situation or discouraging the dilemma, there's always someone out there who is actually in deeper hot water than I am.

I guess this means that I always have two options. I can sit in a corner saying POOR ME, or I can look around to see how the other ninety percent are doing.

And again I have two options. I can gloat and say, "Whew, I'm sure glad it's them and not me." Or I can reach out to try to help those I can and pray for those I can't. I can consider my assets instead of my liabilities, and instead of dwelling on all the things I DON'T have, I can give sincere thanks for all the things I DO have. I can try to develop that ATTITUDE OF GRATITUDE.

Yep, I guess it's obvious that that's what I should be working on instead of sitting around complaining about my cat. So from now on, instead of being jealous because I have to catch colds and he doesn't, I'm gonna be grateful that HE has to catch field mice and I DON'T!

Sound Retreat!

Many people find it peaceful and spiritually rewarding to go away for a weekend prayer "retreat." I had been thinking about doing this for a while, for a while of about five years.

Finally, I got around to making the reservation and planning the weekend. I was told to arrive at the retreat house at six p.m. on Friday. Since I would be working at the office that Friday until five p.m., I packed my suitcase the night before and felt very organized. I put notes on the refrigerator about how to fix dinner, put out garbage, feed cat, etc., etc. By the time I left the house I held my head high, knowing for once I "got it all together."

During the day, I began thinking about the upcoming peaceful days, sitting alone in a room, reading, meditating, maybe dozing, listening to inspirational lectures, eating healthy food.

The thought of food always distracts me into dangerous detours. It suddenly occurred to me that it would have been fun if I had thought to bring along some silly snacks—mints or pretzels or cookies—so I could feed my poor undernourished body as I fed my soul.

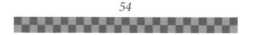

Ah, well, as usual, I had thought of this AFTER I had packed instead of before. But then it occurred to me that I would be passing a grocery store as I traveled the road to retreat! There would be calorie-laden between-meal snacks there just waiting for me to take along as retreat treats.

I left the office right on time, stopped at the grocery store, picked up my gluttonous treats, opened the trunk of the car, slipped them into the suitcase, closed the trunk of the car—and realized I had just locked my car keys in the trunk.

So much for planning and organization.

Luckily, I had learned one small lesson when my son was a toddler and delighted in locking Mommy's keys in the car. I always carried a spare key. But the spare only turned on the ignition. It did not unlock a trunk filled with a suitcase filled with my clothes for the weekend.

So much for calm expectation and peacefulness.

In a wild panic, struggling through rush-hour traffic, missing every light, forced to stop at every corner, I drove the thirty miles home to get the OTHER spare key which DID unlock the trunk. Then dashing madly for the retreat house, I arrived breathlessly late, flustered, and appearing totally disorganized as usual. Tranquillity is not my life.

Dear Lord, how am I ever going to adjust to sitting around on a cloud in heaven when I have had no training for such a life? Without a crisis every fifteen minutes, what will I do all day?

Are you going to arrange some heavenly hassles just so I'll feel at home? Yes, Lord, I know that sounds presumptuous. I may never make it to heaven, but I'm HOPING. After all, I

DID finally make that retreat, didn't I? And I even learned a lesson—that you should not take detours on the road to retreat!

Help me stay away from detours in the rest of my life too, Lord. Surely you've noticed how I plan to go to church during the week, but I stop to straighten the kitchen and put out the trash and throw in a load of wash and then the phone rings and all of a sudden it's too late to make it.

I resolve to set aside time every day to read the Bible. I sit down with the Bible but pick up the newspaper, thinking I'll quickly glance through it first. Then I spot an ad. This reminds me to add something to my grocery list and then I start to look for the coupons I had saved to take along to the store and when I finally find them, they're with the library book that's due back TODAY and I dash off to the library, and it's so long, Scriptures.

Lord, forgive my fragmented mind and give me some stick-to-it-iveness. If that superglue can hang a man by his helmet or hold a car in midair, you must have some kind of God-glue that could stick me to a spot long enough to get me on speaking terms with Scripture.

Lord, thank you for my busy life. I love it. But teach me to not lock keys in trunks and not lock you out of my schedule. Help me to find time to retreat every day, Lord, a time for just you and me.

And, Lord, please don't give away that little spot in heaven that has my name on it. I just might find the road there yet—if I can pass up all the detours.

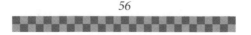

How Can I Worry About Washington and the World-at-Large When There Are Carpenters in My Bathtub?

The other day I was telling a friend about one of my many guilt trips. I told her how I had read the evening paper and watched the six p.m. news. There were terrible tragedies and crisis situations in many parts of the world. I was interested and concerned UNTIL I glanced across the TV room.

Remodeling was in progress at my house, and the carpenters had torn out one of the toilets and thoughtfully placed the pot next to the potted fern in the corner of my TV room. Somehow this disrupted my concentration.

I looked around me. The carpenters had ripped tile off the

bathroom walls, causing a fine powdery dust to float and settle everywhere. It was on the furniture, the floors, the food. It was in the heat vents, on the drapes, and in my hair (in more ways than one). The whole house looked like it was going gray before its time. I KNEW I was!

I fretted, I fumed, and then I remembered the six o'clock news, the problems, the world crises. How could I have forgotten so soon and switched to worrying about something so trivial?

I asked my friend why I was so self-centered. She knew that GUILT was my constant companion so she consoled me. "It's because the toilet in the TV room is REAL. It's here. It's now. It's not six thousand miles away or a vague threat of something that might happen in the future. This Is Your Life, As YOUR World Turns. It's NOT Search for Tomorrow."

Wow! She was right. Maybe I should listen to her advice more often. She's always been a good friend, but maybe she can also be my Guiding Light!

Dear God, if this is my life, help me to get the dust off it. I guess I have to be a little self-centered just to keep my house and my family going, but don't let me so easily forget the OTHERS with problems larger than mine. Help me to do what little I can to change what I can. Give me the perseverance to participate, to protest, to protect, what I believe in. Help me to do small things since I can't do large ones. Help me to reach from my small world and learn a little more each day about YOUR wide world. And thank you, Lord, for letting me be part of it.

Make Room
for Room Mothers

oan of Arc, Molly Pitcher, Florence Nightingale, and all those other heroines might be in the history books, but none of them ever had half the courage and stamina of a twentieth-century woman who volunteers to be a ROOM MOTHER. Now there's true grit.

Joan of Arc had her armor to protect her. A room mother, without armor, has to ride on a school bus full of little bodies bent on destruction.

All Molly Pitcher had to do was carry pitchers of water. Room mothers have to mix, serve, and wipe up spills from pitchers of sticky fruit punch for class parties.

Florence Nightingale just had to withstand battle fatigue and maybe the plague. Room mothers are exposed to colds, coughs, measles, flying lunch boxes, kicks in the shin, and bubble gum in the hair.

For years, I staggered along on field trips, exploring the joys of pumpkin patches, historic sights, state parks, museums, and even an Indian burial ground. One time we lucky room mothers got to accompany the class on a trip to the riverfront

and a cruise on a riverboat. Joan, Molly, and Florence would never have survived the terror of wondering which kid would fall in the river first or which room mother would abandon ship first.

At that point in time, my son had a darling little girlfriend. Everyone on a field trip always has to have a "partner," so if one gets lost, the partner can point toward the dog the lost person was last seen chasing. The girlfriend announced she would be MY partner.

My son's best friend was HIS partner, and we all ended up sharing a table on the deck for lunch. The girlfriend kept staring at my son adoringly and smiling at me and murmuring, "Doesn't he say the cutest things?" My son was only in the FOURTH GRADE, and here I was with the beginning symptoms of mother-in-law-itis. I don't know what ever happened to that little girl, and she will never know how close the room mother came to stuffing a caramel in her braces!

The day we went to the Indian burial ground, I was fascinated by the Indian artifacts and the burial customs described in a short film. The children were fascinated by a muddy field nearby and the challenge of seeing who could transfer the most mud the fastest from field to kid. When we left, the field was bone dry and every mother's washing machine was doomed to a mud-overload cycle that night.

Another time we were scheduled to take a train ride. We spent an overstressed hour waiting for the overdue train and after we finally boarded, the whole trip lasted fifteen minutes! During those fifteen minutes, each kid had fifteen drinks from the water fountain, stepped on the toes of every passenger in an aisle seat, ran in and out of the bathrooms, tried to pry the windows open in an effort to fall out of them, and convinced the conductor he should take early retirement. Not one of the children had

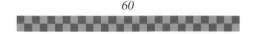

ever ridden on a train before. Not one of the mothers will ever want to ride on one again.

Heroines of the past, step aside. The true stalwarts are the twentieth-century room mothers who get bunions from Scout hikes, indigestion from hot dog buffets (!), and laryngitis from shouting, "Line up NOW...only two cookies per kid...sit still...be quiet...and WHY do you have your foot on that little boy's head?"

***

Dear Lord, could I resign from the room mothers' sorority and just run away to become a missionary in the jungles of Brazil instead? That sounds so much simpler than suburbia.

In this traumatic twentieth century, we may not go off to fight noble crusades, but we fight the battle of committees and church socials and class parties and baseball schedules that change and school buses that don't come and traffic that jams and taxes that come due. We fight frustration, every day.

Lord, we fight a war without medals.

Dear Lord, help me to have the courage to fight the battles I should, the prudence to stay off the committees where I don't belong, and the wisdom to know the difference.

And, Lord, the next time someone suggests I volunteer to be a room mother, remind me to put my "nos" where my mouth is.

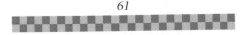

Do You Hear Me, Hear Me?

Why does my husband think we live in an echo chamber?

I say to him, "Do you want the window closed in there?" He says, "In there?" I say, "Yes, in there." He says, "Yes." I say, "Do you want coffee now?" He says, "Now?" I say, "Yes, now." He says, "No." I say, "Do you want a divorce or a hearing aid today?" He says, "Today?" I say, "Yes, today." He says, "Maybe later."

I don't mind saying to kindergartners, "Repeat after me." But I thought my husband would have outgrown that by now. And besides, I didn't say to him, "Repeat after me." If I had, he would have said, "After you?"

I think I am definitely going to have to do something to try to improve our communication system. Maybe I'll start writing him notes. Or maybe I'll enroll us both in a sign-language course. Or maybe I'll give him a chance to find out how it feels to live with echoes—I'll buy him a one-way ticket to the Grand Canyon!

Dear Lord, do you think my husband echoes because he really doesn't hear me? And do you think that's because I talk to him so much that he's gotten tired listening? NO, it couldn't possibly be that! There must be some other explanation.

Maybe he's just thinking of something else, and the echo gives him time to come back from wherever his musings have taken him so he can realize what I said. Or maybe he doesn't REALLY listen to me anymore, and maybe I don't listen to him either. Maybe we've gotten so busy, working and worrying and wondering what's going to happen next, that we're always slightly distracted. Help me, Lord, to start working on that, to REALLY listen to him so that maybe he will return the favor.

But, Lord, if that doesn't work, you will help me find some way to get his attention, won't you, Lord? Won't you, Lord? Won't you, Lord?

The Match of the Century— Motormouth V. Motorized Machinery

Some people seem to think that machines are going to take over and run the world. They don't know what they're talking about. It'll never happen. Machines don't WANT the world. They just want to IRRITATE the people who are trying to run the world!

I'm sure that in executive suites across the globe, there are business leaders, movers and shakers, and multimillionaires who are, at this very minute, teetering on the brink, wringing their hands, and tearing their hair, shouting, "Find me an empty planet, and send my computer there!" The plan for world peace, the cure for all known disease, and a way to lose weight without dieting are all probably out there somewhere, lost in a computer's memory bank!

But all those important people in that big, wide, wonderful world of high finance and high anxiety who think they've got

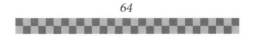

trouble have no idea what it's like back here in the domestic world. Machines have just STARTED running the business world, but they've been running the kitchen for years. Take the stove, the refrigerator, the garbage disposal, the dishwasher. Yes, take them, please!

In the last six months, almost every time-saving device in my house has decided to save time, but not MY time. All I have done is SPEND my time trying to get them to work! All they have done is smirk and giggle, saying, "Look at the funny human!" They are so smug when I moan and groan, kick and shout and try to get a Doctor of Appliance to make a house call.

The machines love it. They just sit there, staring at me as I self-destruct. They don't stir a kilowatt or whirr a motor. They don't CARE about all the years we have spent together.

But if you think those monsters want to take over the world, just think again. Consider. If you would take the average person and stick his or her finger into an electrical socket, you would definitely get his or her attention, wouldn't you? But my machines can suddenly stop working and go sound asleep while

their cords are plugged into electrical sockets! Does that sound like the kind of dynamic force that wants to rule the world?

No, no. Machines will never take over. They know it's a lot more fun IRRITATING the world than trying to run it!

———⚜———

Dear Lord, are you giggling and smirking just like my appliances? I guess you think it's pretty silly for a grown woman to get so shook up over a few malfunctioning appliances. And, as usual, you're right!

I don't need a stove. I can build a fire in the backyard and roast hot dogs. I don't need a dishwasher. I can use paper plates and then toss them into the fire. I don't need a freezer. I can pour the melted ice cream into glasses and try to convince the family we are having milk shakes.

No, I can't, Lord. Don't let them find out that I NEED those machines. They may not want to take over the world, but they make a world of difference in my kitchen. So thank you, Lord, for my appliances, lazy though they may be this week. Those machines may be irritating, but I've grown accustomed to their interface!

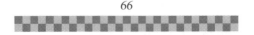

My Car Brakes for Antiques—They Make Me Feel So Young!

To the casual observer, the inside of my house looks like ye olde antique shoppe, full of rickety chairs, potted ferns, and charming little "pieces" (translation: objects of unknown origin).

But the more careful observer—my husband—sees it this way: "Why don't you get rid of all this junk?"

Get rid of my junque? Never! Its oldness keeps me young. I can't afford beauty spas, psychiatrists, or exercise salons. I CAN afford junque.

Actually, there are only a couple of REAL antiques in my whole house. All the other stuff from garage sales and junk stores just LOOKS one hundred years old. I like it that way. When I get up in the morning and look in the mirror, no matter how bad the face looks, I know I STILL look younger than the hall tree with the Civil War bullet hole and the ice tongs hanging in the kitchen and the treadle sewing machine and the tintypes and the genuine wicker rocker. They make me feel sooo young.

Today a lot of people love the old things; and if a lovely old mahogany table has a wobbly leg or a charming rocker has a squeak or there are a few nicks or notches here or there, well, that just makes them more loveable.

I wonder why we don't feel the same way about old PEOPLE. As soon as they get a wobbly leg or squeak with arthritis or have a few nicks or notches here and there, they become PROBLEMS. These little defects don't make them loveable. Being old doesn't add to their value.

I know a few old people who are really precious to me and a joy to know, but I only see them occasionally. They don't live with me. There is no one in my immediate family whose age or nicks or wobbles have made them a liability, and since the problem of an aging relative hasn't touched me personally, I can't really KNOW about it or be objective about it. But I see it all around. And it makes me feel sad.

———⟿⟾———

ear God, please help us to appreciate and try to understand the problems of older people. We make allowances for the young and their inconsistencies. Help us to make allowances for the old and their infirmities. Help us to reach out to the alone and the lonely. Help us to remember that we are all different—tall, short, fat, skinny, silly, serious—but we will ALL be old some day. Let this sameness unify us to do all we can to bring warmth and comfort into the lives of our aging friends and relatives who have reached the sunset years.

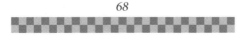

You Are Known by the Company You Keep

I've always wondered about that saying. Does that mean if you have a successful dinner party, you should KEEP the company as long as possible? Are you supposed to have them move into the guest room and see if you can KEEP them longer than the people next door kept their company who came for the Fourth of July and left on Christmas Eve?

Is it better to be known for keeping a little company a long time or a lot of company a short time? Or are you supposed to KEEP a whole business "company"—TAKE AND HOLD HOSTAGE your whole local electric company or telephone company or gas company? Sometimes when I get the bills, that idea appeals to me and with the publicity that would cause, I would certainly get "known" for it. But I guess that old saying really means you are known by the people you hang around with.

I have always had bad luck there. It started with my sister. I only had one, so she was the company I kept, and I always looked

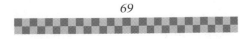

bad as a result. She was so beautiful and sweet and charming that boys practically stood in line to get a date with her. She would actually have two dates in one day—afternoon and evening shifts. I was lucky to get two dates in one year.

When she got married, she had a dream house. Every room looked like a magazine picture from *House Beautiful*. Years later, when I got married, the rooms in my house looked like pictures from a magazine too—the Salvation Army magazine (I bought most of my furniture from their thrift store).

To top it all off, my sister also became a gourmet cook. AND every year she had a huge vegetable garden, where she grew enough lovely edibles to can or freeze into delectable concoctions. With all the preserved goodies, elaborately decorated cakes, and never-ending new recipes, a meal at her house was always memorable. My meals were memorable too—the indigestion would keep you remembering them for hours.

It's a good thing my ideal sister was also one of the neatest, sweetest people in the whole world and I was always crazy about her, or keeping company like that could have been a real drag.

But I never learn. I proceeded to make FRIENDS like that too. Eleanor sang like a nightingale, was so holy everyone spoke of her as the nicest girl in town AND she was so skinny she was always trying to gain weight by stuffing down whipped cream and mashed potatoes, while I nibbled on a celery stick and three limp green beans. Competing with that kind of company could have ruined me. Instead, her friendship was so deep and loyal that it gave me a foundation for the rest of my life. I knew no matter who criticized me for what, Eleanor would always defend me and believe in me and be my friend.

After that, I continued to keep bad company. When I got a singles apartment, Teresa had a singles apartment down the street. We had Sunday morning breakfast every week, tea and

sympathy, toast and therapy. I got married in September; she got married in December. I had a son; she had a son. Then she out-mothered me, by having three lovely daughters. In spite of my envy, her intelligence, wit, goodness, and creativity have continued to amaze and sustain me through the years.

There have been so many others—neighbors and relatives, the ladies of my prayer group who share praise and care every week, the people I've worked with—and that includes men friends as well as women.

And then there is Mary Clare, beautiful, talented, important, stylish, and shortsighted enough to like me a lot. Together, we've traveled through Europe, double-dated, survived the advertising world's woes and wonders, partied and mourned and rejoiced and talked for 7,744 hours (estimated at one hour a day since we met, a very low estimate). Next to her, I always look bad, but with a friend like that, it's worth it.

If I am known by the company I keep, then I am dynamite!

—⌒⌒∾⌒—

ear Lord, thank you for blessing me with family and friends who are such good company. Help me to remember to be kind to those who are less blessed. Remind me to take time to talk to people at meetings or parties who seem to be lonely or alone. Help me reach out to those who might not seem like good company but might just need a little friendship to get them going. As I exult and delight in my friends, Lord, help me remember there is only ONE friend I truly need. Thank you, Lord, for the pleasure of YOUR company.

The Secret Closet

D o you have a secret closet, filled with an entire wardrobe that only exists in your imagination? I know I certainly do.

My real-life wardrobe is pretty average. My husband sees me shuffling around the house in the morning, wearing an old threadbare bathrobe and fuzzy house shoes that look like a porcupine that got blown through a wind tunnel and went limp.

The neighbors see me putting out the garbage or digging in the flower bed, wearing an old pair of slacks with a hole in the knee and a loose striped top that is so faded and pitiful that it looks like it must have been made from Ringling Brothers' first circus tent.

And when I have lunch out with friends or go to church, I am wearing the usual uniform—a conservative skirt, blouse, jacket, medium-heel shoes, and maybe pearl earrings.

But in my imaginary secret closet, there's a full-length red sequin evening gown, strapless, with matching shoes and a feather boa! There's an elegant black riding habit with jodhpurs, shining black leather boots, and a little black derby hat. There's a bright-blue-and-white-striped yachting outfit and a bright yellow, full-skirted, organdy garden-party dress with a picture

hat. And there's an Amelia Earhart aviatrix costume, complete with a long white scarf to flow in the breeze as I take off in my open cockpit plane, waving to the admirers who have gathered to bid me bon voyage as I leave to set a new record as the first woman to fly to the moon in an open cockpit plane.

Ah, yes, that closet is filled to the brim.

I don't know why that humdrum, ho-hum hausfrau has been masquerading as me, myself, and I when the woman who wears the clothes in that secret closet is the REAL me!

$\sim$ § $\sim$

ear Lord, you and I both know that only YOU know who the real me is. I never have found out and maybe never will. But I'll keep looking for me. In the meantime, all I do know is that I'm not any one of the women who would wear the clothes in my closet. Instead, there's a little bit of each of them in me, some struggling to get out, others content to keep it quiet. And that DOES make for an exciting though confusing life. So, thank you, Lord, for all the "me's." And it doesn't matter if I ever find out which is the REAL one. Just help me to be what you want me to be.

And if I never get to wear that red sequin dress in real life, Lord, maybe I'll put a request in my will that they dress me in red sequins for my final "So Long." That would be one sure way of making a memorable exit, and it would make everybody else start to wonder, as I have, "Who was that woman anyway?"

The Whys Will Inherit the Earth

escendants are deflating to the ego and hazardous to your mental health.

When my descendant was about six years old, he had a million questions and I had answers for all of them. His whys didn't bother me because I either knew the answer or could make up one that was satisfactory to the six-year-old intellect.

And then he began to grow in age and wisdom.

In normal, everyday conversations, he started to slip in such questions as: "Why does breaking the sound barrier make a noise? How does a quartz watch work? What do you think of the theory of thermonuclear plasma turbulence?"

Actually, these questions weren't more profound than his earlier ones: "Why is grass green instead of blue? Do spiders drink water? Why can a dog run faster than a man when a man's legs are longer? Are angels' wings made out of feathers like birds or skin like people? Do gerbils have a sense of humor?"

There was only one big difference. When he was six, I had answers and he thought I was wonderful and intelligent and

74

knew everything. But when he turned into a teenager, my clever answers turned into BORing and he thought I was silly, stupid, and undereducated.

When I had to start answering, "Well, I never really thought about that before"—or—"That's not really in my area of knowledge OR interest, so I don't know the answer," he looked at me in wonder and disgust and said, "What happened to you? You used to be so smart and now you don't know anything!" I couldn't even think of a clever answer to that.

—⚘—

Dear Lord, you must feel the same way about me sometimes. When I was younger and asked you "Why, Lord, WHY?" your answers always satisfied me. I was secure. God was good. God knew everything and answered all my questions and needs. Like my son, I basked in my Father's omniscience.

Then I began to grow in my "faith experience." My questions got harder, and it seemed your answers were more vague. I asked, "Why is life unfair? Why do we have to have war? Why do people have to suffer? Why do some seem to have more problems than others? Why did the garbage disposal back up the day I was having the bridge party? Why, Lord, why?"

You must be getting awfully tired of the questions of your descendants, Lord. Unlike my son's mother, you, my Father, have ALL the answers, even to the questions I will never be smart enough to ask.

You even give the answers to me sometimes. But I don't always understand them or I don't LIKE them, so I keep asking over again, hoping that I will hear an answer that suits me better next time. Forgive my arrogance, Lord.

I know the growing pains are necessary. I know I have to

keep wondering and searching and asking if I am to grow toward a mature faith. Forgive my yearning for the old security. Help me to enjoy the journey and the never-ending discovery of your dimensions and delights. Thank you for giving me the ability to question, and please give me the patience to wait for an answer.

But, in the meantime, Lord, tell my kid that he has contributed ENOUGH to my spiritual growth! I now have enough humility and loss of ego. Please make him think of some questions that I DO have answers for. Only you, Lord, are powerful enough to do that.

A Rose is a Rose is a Thorn

E very time you think there is something for sure you can count on, you can't.

Nothing is forever for sure anymore. Once upon a time, you lived in the same house for years, maybe even a lifetime. You kept the same spouse forever, you knew the same people and had the same friends from grammar school on. Now it's move, change partners, pitch out but never pitch in.

Even something you think you know pretty well—like your husband—is subject to change. Last week we went out to dinner to a fancy restaurant to celebrate our anniversary. It was so fancy they didn't have a menu. The waiter explained the selections available for each course in glowing phrases.

As we sipped a drink, he approached and began to describe the appetizers for the evening. I smirked inside, knowing that he was wasting his time. Not once since we

have been married has my husband opted for an appetizer or even nibbled on a single hors d'oeuvre.

Without a moment's hesitation, my husband ordered oysters on the half shell. The waiter assumed I didn't wish to order anything since my eyes were bugged out and my face was turning red as I spluttered and coughed from the olive I had just swallowed. Noticing my surprise, my husband said innocently, "I LIKE oysters."

The salad was next and my lifetime partner, who has never allowed me to taint a single lettuce leaf of his with anything but French dressing, chose the HOUSE DRESSING.

But the entree—aha—I knew I knew him there. We could be stranded at a Hawaiian luau or in the middle of a Mexican fiesta and he would insist on a steak. This restaurant offered only a few entrees, but one of them was beef, so I knew he would order that. He ordered the pork.

I was afraid to go to the ladies' room to powder my nose. Since he had obviously just been stricken with a severe case of change, I was afraid he would change tables while I was away.

Dear Lord, sometimes I feel the same way about religion. It all seems to be changing too fast for me. Morals and values I thought would never change seem to have new "inter-pretations." Old songs have been replaced with new ones. Quiet organ music has been replaced with guitars, flutes, and synthesizers which clear my sinuses but are not always my idea of proper accompaniment for a heavenly choir.

Help me, Lord, to hang on to your "old" commandments and teachings and at the same time be open to new ways of

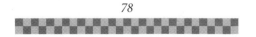

praising you, ways that may be more meaningful to others than they are to me.

Help me remember the sunset that is always the same but never the same two nights in a row, its brilliant colors and soft shadows always shifting and changing. Help me remember the rose bush by the patio. Each new rose is always pink but never the same pink. Every petal is subtly different with endless variations in color and shape. Remind me of the ever-present clouds, white and fluffy and fleeting or gray and brooding and mysterious, constantly making new patterns and designs, never the same from one moment to the next.

Your creations are never static, Lord. Why should your people be? You are always the same, Lord, always loving me, but the ways you manifest yourself are infinite.

Thank you, Lord, for the challenge of change, the new horizons, the opportunity to discover new insights into the myriad workings of your plan for the world. And for me.

But, Lord, the next time my husband and I are in a restaurant, if he suddenly orders smoked buffalo or chocolate-covered centipede, I'm heading for a marriage counselor.

The Ten
Most Wanted

The FBI would love my house. It's FULL of finger-prints.

If only their mobile crime detection unit would come by and dust a few for me. They could take care of the ones on the TV room ceiling that I can't reach (my son is tall) and pick up a few from ANY corner or doorjamb. The refrigerator door alone could keep the feds busy for a week.

The members of my family believe in leaving their mark wherever they go. While other people collect Norman Rockwell prints, Grandma Moses prints, and so on, I collect thumbprints, pinky prints, fist prints, and even palm prints.

Did God go to all that trouble to give us each our own special unique set of fingerprints just so they could be left on the hall wall, the basement bannister, and the kitchen cabinets?

Other people can solve their problems by writing to Dear Abby. Evidently, the only way to solve mine is to somehow get in touch with an FBI agent.

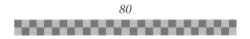

Dear Lord, have you noticed that I spend more time complaining than correcting? Send down a thunderclap that will help me get off my soapbox and get out my soap bottle, so I can go ahead and clean up all those fingerprints and be FREE. Free to daydream and find delight, free to compliment instead of complain.

Help me forget the peanut-butter smudges and the dirty fingerprints and see YOUR fingerprints all around me—the jonquils in the garden; the redbird that visits our patio and flutters about in the birdbath, reveling in the cool water and, obviously, not CARING if he uses the wrong deodorant soap; the high, tinkly giggle of the little girls playing across the street; the fresh, earthy smell of the green beans I am snapping for dinner; and the warm earth and cool grass under my bare feet. Ah, yes, Lord, your fingerprints are everywhere. And I don't need the FBI to help me identify them!

Getting it in the Neck

The Empress Eugénie of France sure had a lot of class. One day she was ailing with a bad cold and a sore throat when her husband, Napoleon III, asked if he could get her something for her throat. She answered yes, and told him just what it would take to make her throat feel better. He sent right out and got it for her.

It was a diamond necklace they had seen the day before at their friendly neighborhood jewelry store!

Last week I was ailing with a sore throat, and my husband asked if I needed something for MY throat. I answered yes, I thought maybe some cough lozenges would help.

He said, "Well, why don't you get some when you go out to pick up my suit at the cleaners? I have to have that suit TODAY."

I think the Empress Eugénie had something I don't. She had a commanding presence that got her the royal treatment!

ear Lord, I think my husband has me by the throat. What makes him think he can tell me to run errands when I have a sore throat? Oh, well, it could have been worse—I could have had a sore foot!

Actually, he's usually very solicitous and understanding. He just doesn't think a sore throat is cause for invalidism, and I guess it's not. But, Lord, since I didn't get the lozenges and I don't think there's any chance of getting a diamond necklace, maybe tonight I'll groan and moan and clutch my throat. Then I'll tell him about the Empress Eugénie—AND about that beautiful turtleneck sweater I saw at our friendly neighborhood clothing store. If I don't get the royal treatment after that, HE'S the one who's gonna get it in the neck!

Will the Bluebird of Happiness Nest in Your Neck Wrinkles at Age Forty and Even Beyond?

keep waiting for it to start. They say life begins at forty, so it must be around here somewhere.

I read an article that said this was a dangerous age so you should become a NEW you, try something different. I got a facial and a new hairdo and asked my husband if he thought I looked different. He said, "Yeah, you do. Are you coming down with the flu?" I sprayed myself with a new perfume and he asked if something was burning in the kitchen.

I got out my old Spanish dictionary and decided to surprise a long-time friend who had been in my high school Spanish class. I called her and cheerily said, *"Como esta usted?"* She huffily replied, "Wrong number" and hung up.

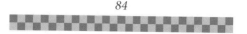

I got out my French cookbook and made *boeuf bourguignon* for supper and my son took one look and said, "Stew again?"

I guess I could take yoga lessons or join a mud wrestling team or try to learn to play the marimba—and maybe life would "begin." But I've had enough trouble—and a lot of fun—with the life I've already begun so I don't think I'd want to return to go and begin all over again! Besides, even if I became a new me, probably no one around here would even notice. So I guess we're all just going to have to be satisfied with the old me.

---

ear God, they say crow's-feet and laugh lines give you character. I've GOT the crow's-feet and laugh lines, now how about helping me develop the character? Help me learn more about maturity and yearn less for youth. Help me to remember, "You're not getting older, baby, you're getting better"—but instead of in the usual translation, in the way YOU translate "better." Help me to be good. Help me to gentle my reactions. Help me find time to learn more about ME, and mine. Who knows, maybe it'll work. With all those crow's-feet, the bluebird of happiness should feel right at home.

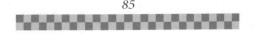

Santa's Been Framed!

You've probably seen pictures illustrating the ages of man and/or the stages of man, but I have a picture frame in my family room that perfectly depicts the stages of Santa!

It started when my son was about three years old and we began the yearly ritual of visiting Santa. Now, I didn't go about this haphazardly. Every year we went to the same place to sit in the same chair, and even saw the same Santa most of the years! And it was always a great and wonderful adventure—for me! As for my son, well, he had mixed feelings about it.

The Santa station I chose for us to visit was at a department store that always has a fabulous Christmas display that's like walking through a winter wonderland. One year it was designed like an old-fashioned Christmas. As we walked along, we saw scenes with animated figures dressed in yesteryear's clothes, skating on a mirrored frozen lake, baking Christmas cookies on a black iron stove, singing carols, and decorating a Christmas tree with strings of popcorn and cranberries.

Another year it was all animated animals, dancing bears, singing chipmunks, squirrels dashing up trees and bunny rabbits hopping out from behind bushes, all busily doing

"people" kinds of things, like wrapping gifts, getting tucked into bed, and wearing red flannel pajamas to await Santa's arrival. But the year that was my son's favorite was the computer year. That display featured rooms of Santa's workshop, but it was all very modern. Everything was made of shiny foil, and there were computers with brightly colored buttons and blinking lights and puffs of smoke. Santa's elves were busily turning out toys, packing gifts, and of course, making lists and checking them twice—all by computer!

That year my son's eyes got as big as saucers as he studied every detail, and I had a terrible feeling that the little wheels in his little head were spinning like crazy as he tried to figure out how he could go home and make something just like that in his own basement workshop. And I was right. He spent most of the next year trying to build a basement computer out of string, cardboard boxes, pieces of broken toys, and some rolls of adding machine tape someone had given him.

But EVERY year was Mommy's favorite. I loved every blinking, nodding, snow-covered, fantasy-filled part of every single display. And when we came to the end of our journey through wonderland each year, there was a special little room for the kids to go in to visit Santa and to have their picture taken. And that was the part of the program that was not always well received.

The frame in my family room holds six pictures, taken six years in a row, in that same room in the same chair. And I think they capture the stages many children go through with Santa.

In the first picture, my son, age three, is wearing the cutest little snowsuit, but his cute little face is just beginning to pucker into a full-blown scream of terror as he realizes he is sitting on the lap of a strange man with a big white beard. The next picture shows a more mature four-year-old, wearing a turtleneck

sweater, a cute stocking cap, and a look of cautious curiosity—no tears but still no smile.

But then comes age five, in long pants and dress shirt and a big, beaming smile. (This Santa stuff is beginning to be pretty good.) Age six shows another nice outfit and another nice smile, though this one is a bit more restrained. The smile of age seven is a put-on polite smile for Mommy and the camera (not showing too much enthusiasm, just in case those kids at school were right about doubting Santa's authenticity). And the last smile, at age eight, is a resigned, embarrassed smirk that obviously says, "I'm trying to be nice about this, Mom, but this is the LAST year I am going to sit here on this man's lap."

Well, it was a good six years anyway. And even though we didn't get any more Santa pictures taken, my son and I still go every year to have dinner downtown and to wander through wonderland. He knows it would just ruin Mommy's Christmas if we missed it!

~§~

Dear Lord, thank you for all the ages and all the stages, all the wonderlands and all the wonderful Christmas traditions. And, Lord, forgive us when we get so caught up with the cute chipmunks and Christmas cookies that we seem to forget whose birthday it is. Remind us, Lord, to celebrate and appreciate the true wonder of the day, the true miracle of your coming.

And, Lord, when the time comes that my tall teen can't take time to see Santa any more, would you help me find a place where I can rent a kid to hold my hand through wonderland?

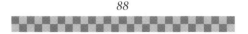

Wild Onions in the Garden of Life

Have you noticed that people are like onions? Especially the people in your family—your nearest and dearest.

They make you cry a lot. Especially when you are trying to get under their skin to get down to the next layer to find out what they really mean or really need or really want.

And they have a LOT of layers. Every time you peel away one layer and think NOW you really understand them enough to have a meaningful relationship, all you find is another layer. Where will it all end?

Sometimes, no matter how much I peel and cry, I just can't seem to get to the root of our pungent problem. Other days, it's just a thin-skin thing and we can get right down to a spicy discussion and settle everything deliciously. And then there are days like today when I start thinking about French onion soup and wondering if maybe the French Foreign Legion is looking for a few good onions!

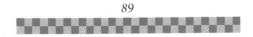

Dear Lord, I complain a lot, but I wouldn't want a hamburger without onions or a life without them either. You made so many different kinds of onions—little green onions, red "gourmet" onions and plain old kitchen-variety onions. I love them all. And I love all the onions in my family too. Of course, they CAN cause a stink and teary eyes over the kitchen sink! But that's only once in a while. The rest of the time they make my everyday stew into French ragout.

Are Holidays Made of Holes and Dazes?

I met my husband on Lincoln's birthday, not on Valentine Day. To be romantic, it should have been under a cloudless sky, on a balmy spring morning, under a cherry tree in full blossom. But, since cherry trees don't bloom in February, it was on a cold, blustery day under a street light where fate had sent us both to wait for a streetcar named DeBaliviere (that was the end of the line).

We were married on the Jewish feast of Yom Kippur, which means Day of Atonement. And there have been a lot of jokes about which of us has been atoning ever since.

My husband's birthday is on Veterans Day, which used to be celebrated as Armistice Day. We sometimes engage in battle even on birthdays and have to negotiate a truce before an armistice can be declared or a celebration begun.

And my birthday is on the feast of Saint Nicholas, the saint who probably never wore a red suit, even though his name eventually evolved from "Sint Nikolaas" to "Santa Claus." According to an old Dutch custom, this is the day you are supposed to wake up to find that Saint Nicholas (or someone)

has left a little gift in your shoe. But all I've ever found there was a dirty sock. Do you think maybe there's something wrong with the way we celebrate holidays at our house?

~⑤~

Dear God, as you and I both know, I make a lot of jokes about my husband. But he doesn't know that because he never listens to anything I say! You and I also know that I am very grateful for the Armistice Day when he was born and the Lincoln's birthday when we met and the Yom Kippur when we began atoning and quit lone-ing it. I also want to thank you for my Saint Nicholas birthday. I may never find anything in my shoe, but I find many gifts in my life, and I know they don't come from Santa Claus. They come from you. I believe in you. I trust in you. And I thank you.

And I can hardly wait to see what's going to happen at our house on Groundhog Day!

The Lower Level

Some people can lay claim to having collected a healthy stock portfolio, some first editions, a few priceless art works and a promising future. All I can claim is the collection in my basement.

In other words, whatever item I have collected in the past ten years has been stuffed into the basement.

Whenever there's a need for a last-minute gift, a pot to give a needy plant a home, an outfit for a costume party, or an unusual something for a school project that's due tomorrow morning (the school need having been announced at 10:01 p.m., one minute after the neighborhood store closed), you can usually find it or a reasonable facsimile in my basement.

One time a neighbor and I got ambitious and held a garage sale. I valiantly cleaned out and brought out for sale everything I thought was dispensable. The garage was full and the basement was a little emptier.

The customers came early and bought freely. But then a sweet little lady said, "I don't see any aprons. I was hoping to find some pretty aprons…"

"Aprons?" My greedy ear heard the possibility for another sale. "Just a minute," I said, and dashed to the basement.

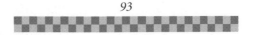

I had remembered the pretty aprons my mother had made and sent me. My mother's neighbors used to tease her that she looked dressed up even when she was putting out the garbage. Whenever you arrived at my mother's house, she always had on a nice crisp housedress, her hair was combed neatly, and she was wearing lipstick and a smile. When she cooked, she put on a pretty apron to stay neat.

Whenever you come to my house, I have on last year's out-of-style slacks and the sweater that shrunk in the dryer, my hair is "casual," and I may be wearing a smile but the lipstick is usually still on the dresser. It seemed kind of silly to put on a pretty apron to protect THAT. So all the aprons were nicely tucked away in tissue in the basement. The sweet little lady was delighted to take them home with her.

Soon other prospective buyers announced they were looking for odd plates…old diapers…baskets…flowerpots. I didn't disappoint anyone.

For the rest of the day, whatever anyone asked for, I managed to find it in the basement. My neighbor/co-seller was impressed. After that, whenever she needed anything, she'd call me. "Got any dinosaur eggs in your basement? My son needs something for science show-and-tell." "Got something strange and exotic for a centerpiece?" "Got a black tablecloth, a purple bunny, a witch's hat, a plastic carrot, a concrete horse's head?" I never let her down.

Through the years the basement has been my treasure-trove, my hope chest, my safety deposit box, and my nemesis. No matter how much I accomplish or achieve, as long as I have the basement, I can never become too smug or self-satisfied. No matter where I am or what I am doing, there is always that nagging conscience telling me that what I really SHOULD be doing is cleaning the BASEMENT!

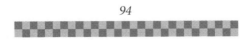

ear Lord, is it just the gypsy in me? Why do I feel the need to collect all this junk? You know I make endless plans to reorganize it, to rearrange all the boxes so no one will notice they are there, to actually throw it all out. But it never happens.

Have you noticed, Lord, how much my life is like my basement? I make endless plans to change that too, to reorganize my days so I'll have more time for prayer, time to exercise and become fit and trim, time to read more books and develop my intellect and go to night school and study the classics and learn how to speak Russian and analyze handwriting and appreciate opera and become a court reporter.

I keep planning to sort out all the questions and problems and answers and solutions and get them packed neatly in labeled boxes for when I need them. But then a new crisis comes along and there I am rummaging madly through the UNlabeled boxes looking for what I need FOR THE MOMENT.

One day a good friend told me, "Life is not to be organized. It is to be lived." I sure hope she knows what she's talking about, Lord. I keep having this vision of approaching you at the Last Judgment and hearing, "Well, you might have made it to heaven EXCEPT you never did get around to cleaning that basement."

Dear Lord, help me to know when it's important to organize and when it's okay to just LIVE. Help me know when to be Martha and when to be Mary. Forgive me my laziness and neglect and rouse me from my stupor in time so I can get everything put up on shelves, off the floor, the day BEFORE the storm sewer backs up instead of the day AFTER.

Thank you, Lord, for the bounty in my basement AND in my life. Thank you for letting me have so much that it NEEDS to be organized. And, Lord, please speak to my husband and tell him divorce court is not the answer just because it's July and I still haven't packed away the Christmas decorations.

New Stations and Different Tracks

Have you noticed how quickly a person's priorities can switch sides? How a new station in life can put one on a new track?

When my son was a preschooler, we had fence-to-fence children in our backyard most of the time. And I became conditioned to shrieks, shouts, and din-in-general as the background music of my life. Then, since most of the kids were the same age, they all went off to school about the same time and, suddenly, all was quiet on the home front. That was when a neighbor and I decided to indulge ourselves in the ultimate luxury—a daytime movie.

Fortified with popcorn, fizzy drinks, and a spirit of wild abandonment, we settled down in the dark theater, ready for the show to start. Just then, a lady came in and sat near us, and she had a small child with her! My friend and I looked at each other in dismay, shook our heads, and moved to another section of the theater. We couldn't stay in the vicinity of a CHILD—it might shriek, shout, din, and disturb! How dare that woman bring along a child to irritate us!

For years, I had to budget so carefully that I would sometimes miscalculate and end up at the check-out counter with just a little too little money to pay the bill, so I would have to decide which item to "put back." This meant the checker had to take the time to remove it from the items to be bagged and deduct it from the bill, and this delayed everybody down the line. Today I have a little more money and a little less time, and whenever that happens to some other budget-bound lady in line ahead of me, I find myself toe-tapping and sighing, wondering why that dumb woman couldn't figure out she had one item too many BEFORE she got in the check-out line. How dare that woman make me wait!

Before I was married, I had a car that was so old that part of the floor was rusted out and I could see what path my life was taking by looking through the hole in the floor. Naturally, the motor was just as old as the floor so it often gasped, gagged, or stopped right in the middle of traffic. I couldn't understand it when the other drivers honked their horns in frustration. Today I still drive an old car, but my efficient husband sees to it that the motor is in good repair at all times so it zips through traffic with the greatest of ease. And whenever I get behind an old clunker that is wheezing and sputtering its way along, getting in MY way, I am furious. How dare that driver delay me.

Isn't it strange how as soon as our station in life changes, so do our priorities? I wonder what would happen if I inherited a gold mine or struck oil in the backyard or got a full-time cleaning lady? I would probably be impossible to live with.

But I sure would like to get a chance to find out!

ear Lord, why is it that we can't ever understand how the other half lives? We strive to move up one notch, and as soon as we do, we forget what it was like one notch below. We can't wait to grow up, but when we do, and have children of our own, we forget what it was like to have growing pains. We yearn to be richer or thinner or smarter or more important; and if we attain it, we have little sympathy for those who couldn't make it. And as we grow older, we forget what it was like at the beginning or the middle.

Forgive us, Lord. Help us to keep striving to do better, to look above and beyond—but don't ever let us think we're too important to look behind or below. Remind us of that famous old saying, Lord: "Be nice to the people you pass on your way up because you may meet them again on your way down!"

What Your Mantra Never Told You!

I f you think a "mantra" is something that goes over the fireplace or that a praying mantra is a weird looking bug with long feelers, then you obviously grew up in a disadvantaged religious school district.

Mantra is a special word (or words) chosen just for you. You repeat your mantra over and over as you sit and contemplate your toes, until some great TRUTH becomes apparent to you or you discover the answer to the mystery of your life.

Now I am not putting down this type of prayer. It is a beautiful and effective way to turn off your motor and get quiet enough for God to speak to you. It is a centering, a focusing, a waiting, a way to let God in. My only problem is in finding the correct mantra for me. I THINK mine might be "cobweb."

Every time I get quiet and contemplate my toes, my mind turns to thoughts of the cobweb in the closet, the cobweb in the back bathroom, and even worse, the ghostly cobweb that haunts the living room. There it lurks quietly in a corner, unseen, invisible to family or cleaning cloth—until COMPANY

arrives. Then the living room cobweb floats hauntingly out into the sunlight, making a specter of itself for all to see.

With all those cobwebs in my head, how can I make room for a mantra?

─⊛─

ear God, help me to shut my mouth and open my heart. Help me to get quiet enough for just a few minutes to forget the cobwebs and company, the dusting and the dithering, and think only of you. Speak to me of the beauty of your world—of MY world.

Help me to LISTEN to you. I am always so busy talking to you, Lord. Let me be silent so you can speak to me. Speak to me, Lord.

But hurry, before the telephone rings.

I Love Me!

I am a wonderful person. I have sterling qualities, naturally curly hair, skinny wrists, nice earlobes, and the inner calm to withstand all the subtle remarks that are slung around my house.

When someone sees something strange growing in my refrigerator and says, "Don't you EVER clean this thing?" I smile. I do not explain that the growth is a new recipe I had originally planned to serve for supper, but considering the way it turned out and the likelihood that my family would turn it down, I hide it in the refrigerator while I tried to think of some way to convert it to an ecologically sound lawn food or a surprise gift for the neighbor least likely to be at home.

I do not explain that before I tried the new recipe, I spent two hours cleaning that refrigerator—two hours that I could have spent reading that new mystery novel I brought home from the library or making lists of smart comebacks to people who do not understand the mysteries of refrigerator hygiene.

I am a wonderful person.

When my husband presents me with an anniversary gift and it is an autographed copy of "101 Fun Facts About House-

cleaning" plus a beautiful bouquet of a dozen red sponges, I smile. I do not crown him with my mop bucket.

I do not explain how that very day I had spent what seemed like 247 hours cleaning house before the kid knocked over the pitcher of juice just as the doorbell rang. I do not explain how when I opened the door, the neighbor's dog dashed in and toured the house. (This dog had obviously just come from an exclusive doggy beauty spa, since she was wearing a mud  pack on her feet.) I do not explain how things like this ALWAYS seem to happen five minutes before Daddy arrives home.

I am a wonderful person.

When my husband and I are having a romantic dinner alone at a restaurant and he looks over his glass and says sweetly, "How old ARE you anyway?" I tell myself he only said that because he is thinking how young and beautiful I look.

When my son says, "You better not have that second donut or you'll get even FATTER" and "Why do you always get your hair cut that strange way?" and "I WISH we could have something good for breakfast sometimes like they do at Jim's house" and "Did you forget to wash my socks AGAIN?" all in a period of fifteen minutes, I tell myself he is going through puberty, so what does he know?

I am a wonderful person.

Maybe I'm not a perfect housekeeper and maybe I could lose a few pounds. But who wants to be skinny and beautiful and live in a spotless house? I DO! I DO!

⸻ ◈ ⸻

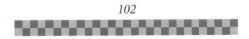

ear God, why didn't you make me a skinny Mrs. Clean? WHY did you make me disorganized and always five minutes behind the deadline and almost-but-not-quite-with-it (whatever IT is)? And why did you make me like chocolate? Dear God, wouldn't you like to reexamine your motives and rethink your original plans for me?

I am a wonderful person, but it doesn't seem to be enough.

Oh, well, now that you and I are both stuck with me, just help me to COPE. Deep down, I know my family likes me a lot. Not just loves me, but likes me too. They complain, but they are natural-born complainers about everything (something else you might have arranged differently!), and I should be getting used to it by now. Thank you for their love and complaints. They keep me "current!" Whenever I let down for a minute, they remind me that there is always room for improvement!

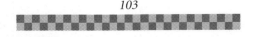

Do Banana Peels and Basketballs Really Belong in the Bathroom?

This morning the neighbors were coming for coffee, so I decided to make a quick check of the bathroom. Either my son had taken a shower there before leaving for school or a basketball team with a monkey mascot had stopped in on the way to a tournament.

There was a banana peel on the sink and a basketball in the corner. I picked up seven, I am not kidding you, SEVEN, wet towels plus assorted clothing and socks from the floor. The bathroom carpeting was  soaking wet, the wastebasket was overturned, and the toothpaste tube oozed its decay-fighting secret formula for all to see, having obviously blown its cap at the sight of the disaster.

If I had asked my son whether he straightened the bathroom, he probably would have said, "Sure I did. I always do." And it would have been an honest answer.

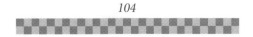

He's a nice kid, as kids go, but a bit absent-minded. One night at nine o'clock, he asked me, "Did I eat supper yet?"

He was the only kid in his class to get a perfect score on his science exam, but that same day he somehow "misplaced" his new watch at school and had no recollection of what could have happened to it. He knows all about the black holes in space that are sometimes called "celestial vacuum cleaners," but he hasn't thought to vacuum his room in six months.

He can discuss Einstein, Isaac Asimov, Dickens, and the Bible. But he can never remember that garbage cans go out on Monday and Thursday, lawn mowers come in out of thunderstorms, and banana peels and basketballs do not belong in bathrooms.

——⚬§⚬——

Dear God, thank you for widening my horizon by giving me a son who marches to a different trombone. Help me to grow with him and for him. Thank you for all the new ideas and fresh insights he gives me, since he views the world from a different angle and is already living in tomorrow while I am struggling to keep up with today. Thank you, Lord, for my son, but PLEASE, could you appear to him in a vision and tell him that dirty socks MUST go in the laundry chute?

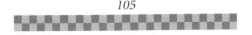

Around the World, Cruising

According to my son, I am about due for a trip around the world! All these years, whenever we have been on our way to a ball game, movie, or school event, I have usually had to stop on the way to do some errand—to pick up a loaf of bread, drop off the cleaning, return the library books, and so on. And I have always said to him, "I'll be right back. This will only take me a minute, and IT WILL SAVE ME A TRIP LATER."

And whenever my son has headed for his hideaway room in the basement, I'd usually stop him, saying, "Wait a minute. Would you take down this box that goes in the storage room?" or "Would you just put this bundle of dirty clothes by the washing machine?" I hate running up and down the basement stairs, so I always excuse these delays with the words, "IT WILL SAVE ME A TRIP LATER."

Finally, the other day, my son said, "Mom, you have saved so many trips that by now you should have enough saved up for a trip around the world!"

Isn't that a wonderful idea? I would have NEVER thought of

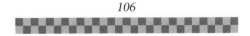

it. But now that I have it, what shall I do with it? Shall I go to Timbuktu or Tangiers, to Australia or Acapulco, to the moon or Miami? Well, maybe someday I'll go to some of those places. But for now, I better get going to the grocery store. I want to get an early start so I'll have time to stop by the gift shop and pick up a birthday present. And then I have to get something for my husband at the hardware store and get that prescription filled at the drugstore. And all those stores are in the same shopping center so if I can get to all of them today, IT WILL SAVE ME A TRIP LATER!

—⁓⁓—

Dear Lord, thank you for a son who thinks off the wall. It makes life a lot more interesting. But all these years, I didn't think about how all my little trip-saving delays were delaying HIS trips, and what he must have thought about that.

Trip-saving is a necessary part of every housewife's life. If she made every trip separate with no on-the-way stops, she'd never get everything done. But of course, he's never been a housewife so how would he know that? In the future, I'll have to try to limit my trip-saving a bit when he's around, but I certainly can't STOP saving trips. How else would I ever get to take that trip around the world?

The Case of the Furry-Hat Attack

My husband thinks he has a cold because he wore a dirty hat. And he calls ME illogical.

Mr. Hatless Wonder usually only bundles up from the tip of his toes to the top of his nose, going out in all weather, shamelessly leaving his curly locks to wave in the cold breeze. But last week, when a near-blizzard hit, he heard that you lose ninety percent of your body heat through the top of your head and decided he'd better try to conserve fuel.

In the back of his closet, he found an old furry hat that someone gave him years ago as a joke. It looked like it might be good for saving head heat, so he put it on and pulled it down over his ears. He looked like a bald eagle with a hair transplant that had run amok. But off he went into the wild, gray blizzard.

Two days later, his nose ran and

his feet smelled. We thought at first that he was upside down, but finally diagnosed it as a cold.

Now, he has always told me that if I would only eat right and get enough sleep I would never catch a cold. But he had been eating right and getting enough sleep, so he had to find some other reason for his malady. He couldn't think of anything unusual he had done that week (like going out in a blizzard), so he decided that the cold facts pointed to the hat.

Obviously, germs had been lurking in that hat for years, just waiting for him to put it on his head so they could attack. He dispatched me immediately to the cleaner to get the offensive hat degermed. They took one look at it and suggested I put it out of its misery, but I insisted they had to degerm it because I couldn't go home without the evidence.

Now my husband is in bed sneezing and snorting and his clean furry hat sits on the shelf, waiting for the next blizzard, waiting for the next chance to attack!

—⚘—

Dear God, what's a wife to do? It's hard enough to put up with all the groans and moans and keep up with the demands for hot-water bags and cold compresses, but now I have to try to keep from laughing at the same time!

Thank you, God, for this serious-minded, life-is-earnest husband who occasionally flips his logic. Life could be so boring without his sudden attacks of irrationality. I mean, even the late late show could not match him for deeply weird originality. So please help me this week to zip my lip and stifle my snickers, as I praise the Lord and pass the chicken soup.

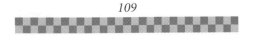

Does 36-24-36 + Equal Zero?

How can you trust a woman who has perfect measurements, terrific clothes, a stylish blonde hairdo, and seems to have a good grip on life? Any normal, slightly overweight woman wearing last year's dress is bound to have an instinctive distrust of such a threatening person.

There was a woman like that in our ladies guild at church. I knew right away I wouldn't like her. I made no effort to be friendly to her or even to stand too close to her. Who wants to be seen standing next to an "after," when you're obviously a "before"?

Then one of my friends invited this glamorous person to join our prayer group, the group that meets at MY house! I was not delighted to hear she had accepted the invitation. She showed up that first day in a great looking outfit that perfectly showed off her perfect figure. The rest of us pulled our baggy overblouses down a little farther over our baggy slacks, tucked our scuffed tennis shoes demurely under us, and tried to smile.

Well, you KNOW what happened. We had to eat our envy. She turned out to be a very nice person who sincerely wanted to

share her prayers and problems with us. And she had PROBLEMS—an ailing mother, a troubled child undergoing psychiatric treatment, a good friend dying of cancer. We soon learned that beauty can be skin deep—but not always.

Dear Lord, teach me to bite my tongue. Remind me that the peacemakers shall be called the children of God, but those with rash judgment shall be called stupid.

It's so easy to envy the beautiful and the rich, Lord, and to distrust them. It's so easy to feel sorry for the poor and down-trodden but some of them live in high crime areas, so we obviously can't trust them either. Then there are the teenagers. Everybody knows you can't trust them. And, of course, the teenagers know you can't trust adults. Who's left, Lord? Discrimination is an equal opportunity employer.

Forgive my distrust, envy, and rash judgment, Lord. Help me to stop being surface-sighted and learn to look inside and above and beyond.

But, Lord, the next time we have a group picture taken, please don't ask me why I am STILL not standing next to my 36-24-36 friend.

The Gold Standard

W hy are goldfish always all a-glitter? There they are, swimming around behind glass walls with no privacy at all! And no matter how far or how fast they swim, they're not going to get anywhere. There's nowhere to go! Not one of them is going to become head of their "school" board or win the Miss Fish contest or have the lucky number in the fishbowl sweepstakes. And yet, they shine and glitter as though theirs was the sunniest job on earth.

I guess God made them that way. All they're supposed to do is sparkle and look pretty so people can enjoy watching them.

I've been thinking that maybe I'm a goldfish too. I sure don't get any privacy at my house. And no matter how far or fast I try swimming upstream, uptown, or up the river, I never get anywhere. I'm pretty sure that I am never going to be chairperson of any board other than the ironing board, and it's a little too late to enter even a near-Miss contest, and I've spent so much money on postage entering sweepstakes that I don't have enough left to buy a new sweeper or even a new broom to make a clean sweep! So what have I got to shine about?

Well, yesterday, the answer hit me like a shining light. I am just supposed to sparkle and look pretty like the goldfish do so people can enjoy watching me be a flash-in-the-bowl. I suggested this to two of my dearest friends, and they both laughed for at least half an hour. I think that must prove my point. I have been put on earth to make people happy.

─◦ରୁ◦─

Dear God, as I am swimming around in my circles, remind me of all the golden things you have put in our world—summer sunshine and autumn apples, lemon meringue pie and lemon-colored kitchen curtains, little girls' golden pigtails and little boys' golden dreams. Thank you, God, for all of them. With such golden glory all around, why should I worry about the fact that my circles are never going to take me anywhere? Who needs to go anywhere else?

Changing (?) Times

I have always been ahead of the times. When other women were wearing short skirts, I was wearing long ones (because I hadn't gotten around to hemming them). When people were just discovering quiche, I had been serving it for ages (except I called it omelet-with-leftovers in a crust).

Well, today I read an article that stated that the American ritual of housecleaning has changed. According to a marketing research group, popularity of "heavy cleaning products" has decreased in recent years. See? They never were popular with me.

While sales of corner cleaners have dropped, sales of air fresheners have increased. One couple is quoted as saying they have switched to forty-watt bulbs so fingerprints won't be seen as easily, and they clean up for company by hiding things in closets. They think this is new? I've always used air fresheners and forty-watt bulbs. And I thought EVERYBODY cleaned for company by running through the house, gathering up everything in sight, and stacking it in a corner in the back bathroom!

The research group interviewed one lady who said her

mother had always cleaned EVERYTHING EVERY week, even to the point of removing every book from the bookshelf and dusting it. The daughter felt that if her mother had used all that energy for some other type of work, she could have been a great executive. There again I was ahead of the times. I have evidently saved YEARS by hardly ever removing and dusting the many books on our many bookshelves.

But something must have gone wrong somewhere because, in spite of all that saved time, I didn't become an executive. And there's one other thing that bothers me. If I am so ahead of the times, why am I always running late?

Dear Lord, for a housewife, a minute saved is not a minute earned. Don't these research people know that? Don't these people know that if you save time by not dusting books, two seconds later a wild and crazy dust storm will suddenly blow up from nowhere and, before you can close the windows, every surface you have just dusted will need to be REdusted. Then the phone will ring and ring and ring and when you dash to reach for it, you will knock off the bag of pine cones you just gathered from the yard for a friend's craft project. By the time you have gotten rid of the salesman on the phone and crawled under and reached behind every piece of furniture in the kitchen to reclaim the pine cones, no one will ever know you saved all that book-dusting time!

And, of course, that little misadventure will make you late leaving to go to the grocery store, and then you will get in the nonmoving checkout line, and this will make you late picking up the kids after school, and this will make you late getting home to put up the groceries and start supper. And then your

husband will come home and say, "Why is supper late? What did you DO all day?"

It's obvious that no matter how much we get ahead of the times, we will never get ahead of the game. Oh, well, what difference does it make in the long run, Lord? The world won't stop whirling whether we're ahead or behind. And, speaking of whirling, I better get busy hiding things in closets, turning on those forty-watt bulbs and whipping up that "omelet with leftovers in a crust." Who knows? If I hurry, I might even have enough time to read a few pages of one of those dusty books!

Just Because Somebody Else's Name Is on the Label of Your Jeans, Do You Have to Stay in Their Hip Pocket?

In recent years, it has been veddy stylish to own jeans, belts, purses, luggage, and even undies that have the designer's or manufacturer's name made into the fabric, sewed into the seam, or somehow INdiscreetly displayed. Don't we have ENOUGH labels? She's a housewife. He's a brain surgeon. She's the wading pool director and chairperson of the cookie sale. He's the executive director and chairman of the board. But let's don't get bitter.

Once I got a dress at a garage sale that looked like it had a designer's label on it, but when I put on my glasses, it turned out to be a cleaner's tag. Oh, well, some of us just aren't the designer type, I guess. We can't really afford to wear only one label when, during the course of an ordinary day, we have to CHANGE

labels from carpool coordinator to stain-removal technician, from garbage-disposal motivator to budget analyst, from corresponding secretary to sanitation specialist.

And the strange thing is that a personality changes as a label does! Sanitation Specialist definitely does NOT have the same personality as Bridge Luncheon Hostess.

Today I was wondering what would happen if I wore a label that said CHRISTIAN that was sewn right into the seam of my jeans or spelled out in dayglo sequin on my T-shirt. Would my personality change then?

If people on the street saw that I had openly labeled myself as Christian, they would expect me to act like one, wouldn't they? Could I handle it for twenty-four hours a day? or twelve? or two and one half? I know some people do. Why can't I?

⌒⑤⌒

Dear God, please help me to pretend today that no one knows what a Christian is, but I am wearing a big label that says CHRISTIAN, so whoever sees me will think that what I AM is what a Christian is. Help me to be loving and giving and peaceful—oh, yes, please, peaceful in the middle of the spilled milk and the not-enough-time. Help me to act Christlike, not ME-like, just for this one day.

Maybe if I can do it this one time, I'll know that I could do it again.

Where's My
Gold Star, Lord?

Every time I decide to turn over a new leaf, something crawls out from under it. One day I decided I definitely must start living more like the women on TV do. I baked some homemade muffins, fixed a tray with my good coffee pot and real napkins, put on a new blouse and lipstick, and called a neighbor to come over and sip coffee like those ladies do on soap operas.

I thought she would come right in the door and give me a gold star for being so charming. Instead, she cringed. "Oh no—how could you? Don't you remember I'm on the green-onion diet? Put those muffins away before my hand reaches out and stuffs one in my mouth!"

I put the muffins away and pretended they were just old leftover muffins anyway. We sipped our black coffee leisurely for eight and one half minutes and then the

cat knocked over a plant and dirt went everywhere, the phone rang, someone came to the door, and my friend suddenly remembered it was THURSDAY, the day she was supposed to be at school helping the fourth graders make Mother's Day presents out of tooth-picks, glue, and sequins. That was the end of that.

Did this discourage me? Yes. But I pulled myself together and continued leaf-turning. I swept and mopped the kitchen floor, discovering dust balls, paper clips, bobby pins, and the earring I had lost two months ago. I was sure Mr. Clean, my husband, would be pleased. I got out a new recipe and fixed a pot of Rich Barley Beef Stew, a meal a man can sink his teeth into. I fixed my hair in a new style with fluffy bangs over the eyes. I took off the new blouse, which now had beef barley spots on it, and slipped into a pretty flowered housecoat.

My husband came home and I waited for my gold star. He said, "What are you doing in a housecoat? Are you sick? Your eyes look kind of funny." Instead of looking at the fluffy bangs OVER my eyes, he was looking at the bags UNDER them.

Then he went into the kitchen. "What are all these spots on the floor? Don't you ever mop in here?" I had not noticed that the bubbly stew had bubbled beef barley spots on the floor, as well as on my blouse. But the stew smelled WONDERFUL, so all would not be lost. We could still have a lovely candlelight dinner just like on TV.

"Why is it so dark in the dining room?" he said. "Let's turn on some lights." When I turned them on, he took one look at the beautiful new recipe. "What is this? You never made anything that looked like this before. Didn't I ever tell you that I HATE barley?"

I did not get a gold star.

I pulled my bangs down farther over my eyes so I would not

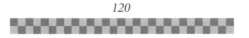

have to watch him picking out the pieces of barley, and I rewarded myself with three homemade calorie-laden muffins thickly covered with butter.

D ear Lord, when I was a little girl, my favorite teachers were always pasting gold stars all over everything I did well. My mother was always so proud of those gold stars. What happened, Lord? Why don't I ever get any gold stars anymore?

Oh, I know my family and friends appreciate me, but not when I WANT THEM TO. I guess you know how that feels, Lord. On Sunday morning, everybody's there at your house, singing songs and telling you how wonderful you are. But on Wednesday afternoon at two o'clock, who's bringing you gold stars then?

Forgive me, Lord, for not praising you ALL the time. Praise and thanks to you, Lord—for sending that gentle shower to water my geraniums when I forgot to do it, for making the birds in all sizes, shapes, and colors so I can watch them out of my kitchen window, for having the imagination to give US imagination so we can think silly thoughts and dream extravagant dreams, for loving us even when we are so fumbling and forgetful. Please accept my gold star, Lord—for the first purple crocus and the last ripe tomato on the vine, for the smell of grass that has just been cut and cookies that have just been baked, for sunsets and dawns and rainbows and the awesomeness of thunderclouds, and for the gift of laughter.

And, Lord, remind me to stop by the store on Saturday and buy myself a big box of shiny gold stars, because it looks like that's the only way I'll ever get any around my house.

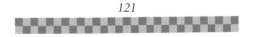

Breaking the Speed Limit and the Sound Barrier

ast year my son and I took a short trip together. We started out early, so on the first lap I drove while he napped in the backseat. And when I saw that long stretch of road ahead of me, I settled down to the monotony of it all and began making lists in my head, as mothers are prone to do—thinking of all the things I had to do, should do, or wanted to do. The longer the list got, the harder my foot pressed on the pedal. Soon I noticed I was going way over the speed limit so I put on my list to pay closer attention to the speedometer.

Then my son woke up and took his turn driving. Things changed quickly. He immediately put on a tape of a rock opera. Yes, opera. It was played by some symphonic orchestra; and we ascended crests as the music rose to crescendos, dropped into valleys as it dipped and swayed, and made enough noise to break the sound barrier. The hills were alive with the sound of our music.

I could tell that my son was NOT making lists in his head of things his mother had told him he had to do, should do, or she wanted him to do. He was totally engrossed in the sound, going with the flow, and lost in the momentum of the music. And soon his foot was getting heavy on the pedal too. Like mother, like son—though, as usual, coming from totally different reasons.

I must confess, though, that his was the better way. Soon I, too, became engrossed in the music—and it was a lot more fun than my lists. He began to point out to me the passages that were his favorites, and it suddenly seemed as though the music had been written to match the scenery we were passing and the cloudy sky and the movement of the car. I never had a more exciting drive.

And since I was there to point out his heavy foot before a highway patrolman did, we arrived at our destination without trauma or tickets. But, although I resolved that in the future I, too, would go with the flow, the next time I found myself on the road, I also found myself making those relentless lists in my head. I guess old habits are harder to break than speed limits or sound barriers.

---

ear Lord, forgive my old habits and help to make some newer, better ones. Remind me that I sometimes go through life the same way I drive—too worried about lists of chores to hear the music along the way, too stuck in my old ruts to try new paths. Lord, help me to learn to go the limit without breaking it.

Different Strokes

W e all have our own idea of an EMERGENCY. At my house, I often hear shrieks of "Oh, NO, it CAN'T be. This is terrible. What will I do?" But when I hear that, I know that the dog has NOT been eaten by a crazed crocodile, our last existing garbage can has NOT been run over by a runaway Rolls Royce, and my neighbor has NOT been kidnapped by an alien spaceship. Such shrieks signal only one emergency. We have run out of root beer.

Would this seem like a disaster to you? Maybe not, but then, what do you know? YOUR emergency may seem equally insignificant to our resident root-beer fan.

My OWN emergencies never seem to even INTEREST the other members of my family. Do they care that company is coming and I forgot to purchase parsley? Do they mind that the girl at the beauty shop totally ignored my warnings, instructions, and invaluable advice and cut my hair ALL WRONG just when I wanted it to look especially nice for the Pothole Protesters Picnic? Do they care that I broke a fingernail just before the bridge club luncheon? What do THEY know about my life and my emergencies?

—⚬§⚬—

Dear God, help me to remember that OTHERS do not always share my feelings or my traumas. Forgive me for expecting everyone else's world to revolve around mine. Help me to listen unto others as I would have them listen unto me. Thank you, God, for letting my emergencies be small, and please help all others who have REAL problems and sorrows in their lives. Let my work and worries be offered up today for them, and in thanksgiving for my many blessings. (And please don't let you-know-who find out that I was the one who drank the last root beer.)

What Do Doctors Know About "Stress Tests"?

When doctors suspect you may have a heart problem, they use elaborate equipment to give you a "stress test." Don't they know that the most effective stress test known to man or woman is being put in a room with a teenager? Clark Kent's "man of steel" bit is nothing compared to the steel nerves required to counter the questions and cope with the logic of the teenage mind. If YOU are seeking the answer to anything regarding school, social life, friends, or the mysteries of the universe, teenage answers will consist of "umnhumn…ughn ughn…gee, I never noticed…how would I know?" If, on the other hand, the teen person is seeking answers, YOU are expected to come up with instant solutions to math problems, where to buy a fifteen-dollar gift that would be perfect for a friend's birthday party, how to get an extra fifteen dollars by Saturday, and Einstein's theory of whatever.

What course on motherhood could have prepared me to answer questions concerning the trajectory of a spaceship, the

warp of black holes, or the wardrobe choices of rock stars. What stomach pill could have saved me from the queasies when, during dinner, I am asked, "Do you guess chicken's intestines have nerves in them?" or "Did this stuff under the onions really come out of a cow's stomach?"

The only way for the average parent to survive the stress test is to try to remember what it was like to be IN that twilight zone, too old to cry or hang on tight to Daddy's hand or let Mommy kiss it and make it well, too young to have any authority or any money or any clout.

Dear God, help me to remember and understand. Help me be strong enough to say no when I disapprove but everybody else's parents are saying okay. Help me to know when it is very important to say yes (even if it is inconvenient) or absolutely vital to stop EVERYTHING and just listen.

Help me to remember that tension comes from two things pulling in opposite directions. Help me to pull FOR and WITH my teenager.

Santa's Mixed Bag

f Rudolph's nose ever has a power outage, I know where Santa can find a new helper. Take my husband, please.

With my husband in the sled, it would be an exciting Christmas for one and all, because every sock would have something in it that was amazing or amusing.

One of the reasons I couldn't resist marrying this man was his talent for presenting unusual gifts. When we were dating, he arrived at my apartment one day carrying an old, wrinkled brown bag. "Here's a present for you," he said.

It didn't look like the kind of gift wrap you'd expect on long-stemmed roses or a diamond necklace, but I took it gingerly and tried to smile. Inside, nestling in tissue, was an exquisite Royal Doulton plate that he had found in a little old antique shop. That plate has been hanging on our dining room wall in a place of honor for years now, and I still love to just look at it and savor the lovely intricate design of the plate and the memory of the day I first saw it.

But then we got married.

One Christmas he gave me an elegant, carved chess set. I don't play chess. He does.

The next year it was a lovely leather case—with a cribbage board inside. I began to wish he'd be less playful.

The following year I expected a silver-plated Monopoly set, but he surprised me by gifting me with a piece of gleaming, honey-colored polished wood, strung with wires. I had no idea what it was but, according to the accompanying instruction booklet, it was an AUTOHARP. I cannot read music. I cannot sing (which you are supposed to do with an autoharp). I asked him if he gave me the harp because he thought I was an angel. He said no.

That was several years ago and so far, even though I briefly tried taking lessons, the only thing I've learned about the autoharp is how to dust it. (Would you believe the only autoharp cleaning method known to modern woman is brushing under the wires with a clean paintbrush!)

BUT the autoharp has taken up permanent residence on the coffee table and has become the best conversation piece a family could have.

There have been other exciting years when I received "interesting" pieces of jewelry and household items, but the best was last year. It has become a matter of common knowledge among my friends that there is one thing that I absolutely CANNOT do, have no desire to learn to do, and will never ever do if I can avoid it—and that is SEWING. I just approach my sewing machine and it starts shooting needles at me and snarling its thread. My son has outgrown clothes before I could figure out how to repair them by mending a small tear or replacing a button. So last year, you guessed it, my husband gave me a large, elaborate, fully equipped SEWING BOX! I know it's the thought that counts, and I sure wish I knew what he was thinking.

I hate to admit it, but do you know I actually LIKE that box?

It's nice to have all my needles and pins and buttons and bows and thimbles and thread under one roof. I may seldom use them, but at eleven o'clock at night I KNOW WHERE THEY ARE.

─◦ॐ◦─

ꗍear Lord, it isn't easy to understand YOUR gifts either. I always seem to get something I didn't know I needed! I asked to be a multimillionaire beauty queen or an internationally famous writer. And what did you give me? A husband I love. A kid I love. A house I love. A job I love. And a lot of crazy fun friends. What kind of gifts are those? What are you trying to do—make me happy?

Yes, Lord, you always know what I need better than I do. I pray desperately for something and you say NO. A few weeks or months or years later I find out how awful it would have been if I had gotten what I was praying for. Thank you, Lord, for so many wonderful unasked-for surprise gifts. Thank you, Lord, for saying no when I need it. Thank you for saying yes even when I don't deserve it. Thank you for knowing me so well and gifting me so generously.

And, Lord, next Christmas, please help me to act more appreciative than appalled when I look in my Christmas stocking and find another surprise!

I'm Only Moving Clouds Today; Tomorrow I'll Move Mountains

'm lounging here on my patio, looking at my bookmark, getting inspired. I mean, isn't that what everyone does? I know people used to turn to the classics and delve deeply into the meaning of life, but today we don't have to do that anymore. I can just turn to my refrigerator and read all the cute, inspirational sayings on the magnets that are clinging there. Then I can look over the comic pages in the newspaper and pick up some food for thought. And then I can look at my bookmarks. It's really simple to get inspired today.

My bookmark has a drawing of a cute, fat, little bear lying on his back in the grass, gazing at the sky. There are little flowers in bloom at his feet, fluffy clouds floating in the sky, and a look of utter contentment on his face. He is saying, "I'm only moving clouds today—tomorrow I'll move mountains."

I love it. I identify with it. I am inspired.

And, of course, I am also too lazy to do anything else today; so this gives me a great excuse to lie on my back and look at the

clouds! Maybe tomorrow I'll move that mountain of dirty laundry and that junk in the garage and that stuff in the closet and those leftovers in the refrigerator.

But today—do you see that cloud to the left that looks like a witch with a wart on her nose, whipping along on water skis…and how about that one right above that resembles a polar bear playing a guitar…and did you spot that one that drifted over a few minutes ago? It looked just like a fat, happy housewife, lying on her back, with her feet propped up on the side of a mountain!

—◈—

Dear Lord, forgive me for putting off until tomorrow what I should be doing today, but even you rested on the seventh day! So I knew you wouldn't mind if I took a day off to admire some of the things you created on the other six.

But, Lord, that reminds me of something I've been meaning to talk to you about. Have you noticed that hardly anybody rests on the seventh day anymore?

Everybody is so busy now with this workaday world that Sunday has become just ANOTHER workday. I know I'm sometimes guilty too, trying to catch up with all the things I didn't get done earlier in the week, busy and bustling when I should be taking a day off to spend with you and friends and family.

Forgive us all, Lord. Help us to remember again that Sunday is a special day—a day to BE…a day to give time and attention to our loved ones…a day to give YOU praise and honor and glory. Remind us all, Lord, that Sunday is a good day to move clouds instead of mountains.